The Instructed Heart

Other OSV books by F. J. Sheed:

Cartoons Catholic (with Jean Charlot)

Theology and Sanity

What Difference Does Jesus Make?

The Instructed Heart

soundings at four depths

F.J. Sheed

Our Sunday Visitor, Inc.
Huntington, Indiana 46750

Nihil Obstat:
Rev. Lawrence A. Gollner
Censor Librorum

Imprimatur:
✠William E. McManus
Bishop of Fort Wayne-South Bend
April 20, 1979

ISBN: 0-87973-629-1 (paperbound edition)
      0-87973-739-5 (clothbound edition)
Library of Congress Catalog Card Number: 79-87925

Design by James E. McIlrath

Published, printed, and bound in the United States of America

TABLE OF CONTENTS

TO MAISIE WARD

This present book has grown out of a paper I read four years ago on the revelations of the Sacred Heart to Saint Margaret Mary Alacoque. It was in effect a study of Scripture's use of "heart," as the organ not only of love but of all our willed activities, hate included. It is intellect and will fused into one principle of action, an instructed heart — which may be a very distracted heart.

I had agreed a year earlier to go to Paray-le-Monial to read the paper. But as September came round, it was clear that my wife was dying. My decision to cancel the journey was the occasion of her last spurt of will, she grew frantic at the idea of my not going because of her. So I went, leaving her in devoted hands in America. I read the paper and rushed back to America — a nineteen-hour journey in eleven vehicles — to hate myself for having left her. She lived another four months in increasing pain.

I have been asked to write a book about her. Unfortunately I am not a biographer, nor am I a portrait painter. But in preparing a book based on the Paray-le-Monial paper — showing the same heart functioning in people today very much as in the centuries Scripture treats — my mind was forced back to the time of its writing and her dying. Gradually I came to feel that a study of one individual heart — and hers was the one I had observed closest — might make a useful introduction to a more general study of the human heart in its relation to God and man. And it would enable me to discharge some of my immeasurable debt to her.

Only some of it. I am writing not as part of the one that she and I became. I study her heart, as objectively as I can, only in terms of this book. I am not writing of our personal relation as wife and husband. She would not want it. I remember a dinner party in Baltimore with a brash young man asking, "Why did you marry Maisie Ward?" and my replying, "We thought it would look better." That was as far as she would have wanted me to go.

In *To and Fro on the Earth* she wrote, "I am grateful for my husband's laughter and my children's." That was *her* limit. *Secretum nostrum nobis,* our secret is our own.

— F.J.S.

One
Particular
Heart

CHAPTER ONE

One Particular Heart

I

Fresh over from Australia, I had known Maisie Ward a few months. She said one day, "I have an idea in the back of my mind." I said, "Your mind has no back." It was my first effort to pin down in words what was to me an entirely new phenomenon; in the next fifty-four years I did not manage to improve on it. You never had to ask yourself what she was getting at or what she was really thinking; she told you. There was no point in searching for ulterior motive, an *arrière-pensée*; her mind had no *arrière*. And with the backless mind went a very expressive face.

She came by her total openness fairly. Her grandfather William George Ward had it. He puzzled everybody with it, set everybody straining for words to describe it. It was not that he could not conceal his thoughts; it never occurred to him to do so. At the oral examination for his degree at Oxford, he certainly puzzled the examiners. Unless he felt he knew the answer fully, he preferred to say, "I have no idea," or, "I know nothing whatever about it." Pressed to take his time, since his failure to answer might be caused by nervousness, he insisted, "Pure ignorance, Sir." Examined a few years later for an insurance policy, he answered the doctor's questions in such terms that he was charged the premium usual for a man of sixty.

His son Wilfrid had something of the same quality, but uncomfortably, often speaking too hastily but very much to his own embarrassment. William George Ward was not embarrassed by it. Neither was Maisie. They both thought that it was normal.

Like most of us, she was stirred by suffering, indignant about injustice. Unlike most of us, she was under a compulsion to do something. Where most people are satisfied with bleating, "This cannot go on," she felt, "It must not." Where our sort say something must be done — she did something. An example occurred before I knew her. During the First World War she was a nurse's aide in a hospital run by nuns who nursed wounded soldiers. Maisie came to the conclusion — wrongly for all I know — that the nun in charge of the actual nursing was being driven to the point of breakdown by a Mother Superior who knew all about superiority and nothing about hospitals. So the nurse's aide went and told her story to the Head Surgeon, who told the Mother Superior, who fired Maisie. She laughed about it whenever her mind went back to it. It made no alteration in her conduct. What she saw, she must say; what she felt, she must act upon. I do not mean that she would rush into action. With the problem of the overworked nun, for instance, she had wrestled mentally for weeks. She could become totally absorbed, not knowing that one was speaking to her. Strangers found it disconcerting. Her family found it hilarious.

Maisie's regarding her sort of directness as normal let her in for a good deal of misunderstanding earlier in life, less as she grew older. In her late teens an aunt had to warn her that a Guards officer with whom she had danced had not understood one word of her conversation about a papal encyclical. She was thirty when I came to know her, but her antennae — I mean the instinctive feel for people's reactions — were still not functioning very vigorously.

I think the last obstacle she had to conquer in herself was the difficulty of realizing that the majority of people did not react to criticism as she did — she listened to it attentively to see what truth might be in it. She spoke her mind to people, *expecting them to do the same to her.* She learnt, the hard way, that they often resented it, as if she were asserting her superiority. This, I say, was about the hardest lesson she had to learn, because it was not in her nature to think herself superior to anybody. She saw every human being as created by God, made in His image, redeemed by His Son. Superiority and inferiority were equally irrelevant. All the same, to the very end, her sheer directness made her impatient if something urgently needed doing — when she showed it too vigorously, she was deeply repentant. As Bishop Eamonn Casey, who had worked with her for years, said at her requiem Mass, "She wasn't above the odd prejudice, but it was based on conviction born of passion and values, and open to conversion!"

To balance the lack of antennae for others' reactions, she had an intense interest in everyone she met; people felt it and confided in her. "Have you ever," she wrote, "made a long journey and fallen into casual conversation with the man in the next seat? . . . And how long was it before he showed you the pictures of his wife and children?" It was forever happening to her. I was once riding in a car with her brother Herbert, she being in the front seat with his chauffeur. Herbert said, "I know nothing of his private life, but by the time we get home she will know all about it." And so it proved. Her instinct was to hold no one at arm's length but to establish a genuine personal contact.

I could fill this sketch with examples. I choose one. She and I met a young priest. He seemed to me rather withdrawn. I forgot about him at once. She did not. At last he told her his tragedy — he was a case of retarded puberty: in fact he had been ordained without having reached it. She took up the matter with his Superior, and he was released to happy laymanship.

Maisie took the Sacrament of Penance with full seriousness. Once, at least, the result was comic. She was staying in a convent and went into the confessional box after several nuns. She confessed that she had had too many cocktails. The priest was startled. "But you, Sister, with your dedicated life! And where did you get them?" He did not find her explanation comic.

This incident reminds me of another, not comic at all, but with one comic moment. She was about to climb the church steps for a midday Mass. A group of boys, charging along in line, knocked her down, her face hitting a step. They went charging on, leaving her bleeding on the ground. She was carried into the presbytery. Before the ambulance arrived, one of the lay staff asked her what they could do for her. She said she would like a whisky. "You surely don't expect to find that here, do you?" was the answer. The thought of a priest's house in which whisky couldn't be found started her sense of humor working. But, in the five years left to her, she never fully recovered from the bruising.

I have met one other person who spoke his mind as she did, never giving a thought to what it might cost himself — the Jesuit Father Thomas Roberts, who was to become Archbishop of Bombay. It was more surprising in him, not only because Jesuits have not that reputation, but more because ecclesiastics generally are not given to taking the laity (or one another, perhaps) fully into their confidence. It is interesting to note that we hear Christ praise only one of the Twelve, Nathanael, and for only one quality — he was without guile.

There is no crime in having a back to one's mind. I have one myself. Indeed, uttering one's mind on a particular matter without weighing all the consequences can mean misjudgment. With the Archbishop it sometimes did, yet I remember him as the freshest wind that ever blew my way from the ecclesiastical heights. With a wind as fresh as that one I had the good fun of living.

The circumstances of Maisie's life gave her an initial width of judgment which the Archbishop hadn't, which few have. She was the grandchild of four Oxford Movement converts. Her father's father, William George Ward, had been an Anglican clergyman. When Newman withdrew to Littlemore, Ward became the effective head of the Movement; priestly celibacy was one of its principles; he startled everyone by getting married (to a clergyman's daughter) and explaining that he was not a priest, since he no longer believed in Anglican Orders. He had his Oxford degree taken from him for writing a book urging England to kneel humbly at the feet of Rome and sue for pardon; with his wife, he preceded Newman into the Catholic Church — and spent his whole Catholic life ranged on Cardinal Manning's side against Cardinal Newman.

Her mother's father was James Hope-Scott, a Movement convert. His second wife was Victoria Howard: her mother, the Duchess of Norfolk, had been received into the Catholic Church by Father Frederick William Faber of the London Oratory, and she and Father Faber between them converted the Duke. All the younger children joined the Church with their parents, but Victoria had to make up her own mind and was received at the Oratory only when she herself was convinced. It reads like a foreshadowing of Maisie: when the pupils at her school were told that they should go to Communion every day, because the Pope was in favor of it, she said she must think about it — one could not just suddenly make as big a change as that. And Maisie was the only member of her parents' circle who wanted Home Rule for Ireland.

II

Wilfrid Ward, son of W.G., tried his vocation to the priesthood, found that he hadn't one, married Josephine, daughter of James Hope-Scott and Victoria Howard. Maisie was their first child.

When asked why he never visited Rome as a Catholic,

Ronald Knox answered, "If you are a bad sailor, you should keep away from the engine room." No family ever lived closer to the engine room than Maisie's. One grandfather taught in a seminary; her uncle was a bishop, her brother became a priest, and several of her aunts were nuns. Old W.G. died about the time of her birth, but his presence was never exorcised. "This family talks as if it had only one grandparent," said her mother.

Wilfrid was born into the quarrel between his father and Newman, which was fundamentally a difference about papal absolutism. W.G. had spoken of the pleasure he would have found in having a Papal Bull at breakfast every morning along with his copy of the *Times*. Like Newman, Wilfrid knew too much history to feel like that. He found himself more and more on Newman's side. He went on to write a two-volume biography of Newman, which stands sixty years after as a kind of Newman *Arc de Triomphe*.

As she grew into her teens, Maisie began helping her father both with the editing of the *Dublin Review* and with his work on the Newman biography. Already she found religion absorbing. Quite apart from her parents' interest in it, she had as chaplain at her convent school Robert Hugh Benson, convert son of an Archbishop of Canterbury, famous for his historical and psychological writings, important to people like me for bringing the doctrine of the Mystical Body back into English Catholic life. She did become, and remained to the end, a daily communicant. She had learnt most of the Gospels by heart; she had begun the reading of the Office in Latin, which was to stay with her till the end of her life, but neither Mass nor Office dimmed her joy in the Rosary. She was widely read in literature generally, French, Italian and above all English — Dickens especially, and Jane Austen and Browning, and Langland's *Vision of Piers Plowman*. She had an astonishing memory — I had memorized yards of poetry myself, but I had not known anyone who could quote prose at such length and with such accuracy. As a publisher I learnt much about the place of reading in the development of the Catholic mind. Without revelation, the reader can know life as he has met it in his own experience and in literature, but he cannot know what life is all about — why man exists, where if anywhere life is leading. He may know what we may call the flesh and blood of life without knowing the shape of reality, knowing a great deal of the parts, but of the totality not a hint. Only too often the theologian is the exact opposite, knowing the general shape but not the flesh and blood. For a balanced knowledge of reality both are needed: Maisie's reading habits had set her on the way to both. Working with her father, she learnt a lot about the need for balance.

The dozen years of Pius X, 1903-14, live sunlit in my own memory. In every Catholic home I visited there was the Pope's portrait, the essence of benignity. His two decisions on the Eucharist — for early Communion and frequent Communion — did marvels for the Church's devotional life. Converts were joining the Church in great numbers, including some who were to become Maisie's closest friends — Ronald Knox, for example. The Pope himself has been canonized. Yet for her and her family the period had elements of nightmare. They were too close to the engine room.

In editing the *Dublin Review* and in writing Newman's biography, Wilfrid Ward was driven almost out of his mind by conservatives of his father's sort, who thought Newman a heretic, and by Newman's Oratorians, who were in a panic lest Ward's account of their founder should cause Rome to declare him one — they controlled the documents he needed for the biography. It would have been a tough situation at any time. The irruption of Modernism complicated it for Wilfrid, and so for his wife and daughter; it brought him to the verge of frenzy.

As a way of thought that Rome saw as a peril to the Faith, the story of the Modernist controversy begins in 1902 with the Abbé Loisy's *L'Evangile et l'Eglise,* in form a defense of Christ's divinity, but leaving little of the divinity standing. For a dozen years the sky was filled with the clamor. In 1906 Pius X wrote an angry condemnation in the encyclical *Pascendi.* More and more writers of what we should now call the Left answered back.

It looks from seventy years after as if to the men of the Curia the peril loomed a good deal larger than life. With some of the extreme "leftists" writing under a dozen or more aliases — Loisy himself using eight — Rome got the impression of an army on the march. It took up battle stations, which often looked like panic stations. Mere accusation of heresy was enough to assure the suspension or dismissal of thoroughly orthodox priests — naturally the poison pen was having a carnival. And some very high ecclesiastics had not enough theology themselves to distinguish between a deeper statement of old truths and their denial.

The outbreak of war in 1914 gave both the world and
the Church other things to think about. The death of Pius X
immediately after meant a new Pope, Benedict XV, aware of
the problems that the Modernists had been making their own
efforts to solve. When six years later I arrived in England, all
seemed to be quiet: the echoes had not reached my teenage
ears in Australia. So I cannot write about Modernism from my
own knowledge. I treat only of what it meant to Maisie Ward.
In the mid-thirties she wrote in *Insurrection versus Resurrection* a couple of chapters on the conflict. Modernism she summarizes as the belief that "dogmas are not the statement of
truths revealed by God but expressions of the religious mind at
the stage to which religious experience has brought it: the
value of dogmas is measured, not by the objective truth of
what they tell us about God, but by the adequacy with which
(for the time being and personally) they express our own
religious consciousness."

In the late sixties she thought of reissuing the book, but
felt that the chapters on Modernism would need rethinking.
And she reminds us that at the time of the conflict she was
very young — she was seventeen when the encyclical *Pascendi*
appeared; her main interest at that time was in the reactions of
her parents.

What turned it all into a nightmare for the Wards was
that some of the Modernists claimed Newman as one of their
own and some of the conservative Catholics agreed that he
was. More than that, many on both sides thought Wilfrid was
a Modernist, on two grounds. First, he held and said that the
problems raised by Loisy and the Irish Jesuit Tyrrell were real

problems and that the official Church was not coping with them. And second, the Wards were friendly with some of the leading Modernists, including Father Tyrrell and Baron von Hügel, who was himself not of them but was the friend and inspiration of many of their leaders: his brother's wife was Maisie's godmother. So the hard-shell Catholics joined in the clamor against Wilfrid, and at moments Rome seemed to be taking them seriously.

Wilfrid was too fine-strung for this sort of warfare on so many fronts. His intellectual grip never slackened, but his nerves were a-jangle, his emotional balance really threatened.

I have said nothing so far about the part played by his wife, Josephine Hope. She seems to have had iron nerves. Her novel, *Out of Due Time,* fine in itself, was exactly the tonic both her husband and Maisie needed. It was based on an earlier break with Rome, that of Félicité de Lamennais in the 1830's. But for both husband and daughter it brought present anguish into better proportion, with the light it shed on the inevitable differences between theologians, concerned to see deeper, and the practical men of the Curia, whose job it was to keep the Church functioning.

In 1912 the Newman biography was published, to be received with an acclaim which in sixty years has not diminished. Soon, with World War I and a new Pope, the special pressures on Wilfrid Ward were over. Within a year of war's outbreak (April, 1915) he died.

Maisie, you may remember, was a nurse's aide in a hospital for the wounded, till she blotted her copybook by speaking the truth. Soon after she found herself concerned once more with the production of a book. A group headed by the vastly learned Capuchin Father Cuthbert, with a number of younger men who were to be prominent in the Catholic intellectual revival just stirring to life, planned a book on the provision God had made by revelation and grace to supply for the insufficiency of the natural order. They asked Maisie to act as secretary to the group. *God and the Supernatural* was the result. She gave me a copy. I was not the only one it set on the way of theology.

What Maisie made of the nightmare years she told twenty years later in the two large books, *The Wilfrid Wards and the Transition* and *Insurrection versus Resurrection*. My interest is in what the nightmare years made of Maisie, especially the effect it had on the element in her which made the judgments out of which action proceeds — the instructed heart, in fact. The distinction between the Church as Christ working through human agents and the human agents through whom He was working was built firmly and finally into the very structure of her mind. She quoted (I think with relish) a phrase from a letter Father Martindale wrote her: "Quite dreadful people do play their right part in the history of the Church, ceasing neither to be right nor to be dreadful." In her small book, *St. Catherine of Siena*, she puts it very clearly, "Too much awareness of the defects of Catholics (especially Catholics in high places) tends with most of us to dim our realization of Christ working mightily through his Church. . . . But with Catherine the appalling evils in the lives of so many ecclesiastics seemed only to highlight her vision of the glorious thing they were profaning."

"The devotional life of Catholics is the essential thing for which all the rest exists." Devotion Maisie saw as our lived relation to God, the heart's response to the reality God has revealed, dogma in action in us. That being the Church's primary concern, Maisie insisted that "the official Church is called on to intervene in the secular order only because the laity is not doing its part."

Having lived through the difficult years, she was not likely to be starry-eyed about ecclesiastics high or low. But she went on to spend close on fifty years bearing witness to the Church on the outdoor platforms of the Catholic Evidence Guild.

III

One day her brother came home with the news that some Catholic laymen headed by a man from New Zealand were defending the Faith in Hyde Park. Leo joined them. So did Maisie. So, a few years later, did their mother.

For Maisie it was a life sentence — forty-eight years under the open sky. Her friends marvelled at her for doing it; she marvelled at them for not. She could see no way out. Millions of people lacked the gifts of Truth and Life that Christ wanted them to have. She must at least *offer* them gifts which meant everything to herself. If people were starving for bread it would be unthinkable not to bring them bread. But this was the bread of life: unthinkable simply to use it for one's own nourishment while millions starved.

She tells of her first effort in Hyde Park — saying she hardly knew what, then running down Park Lane, crying she knew not why. To the end of her speaking life — late in her seventies — she was nervous as she mounted the platform, indoors or out. By the time she had said "Ladies and Gentlemen," she was in complete control. She loved the cheerful songs we made up about our work, especially one ending:

> *And if by our teaching our crowds we mislead,*
> *At least we are orthodox saying the Creed.*

Maisie gave the whole of herself to every crowd, large or small. She would talk happily to half-a-dozen people. If no one at all was there, then she would go on talking to no one at all — a dreary occupation, that; she would keep talking as long as there was any hope of persuading some of the passers-by to stop. An essential part of her character was her reluctance to take "no" for an answer. Surprisingly often it turned out that "no" was not the answer. And she prepared as thoroughly for a London back street as for a university audience — the degree of preparation is concerned with the subject matter, divine Revelation, not with the meeting place.

The Catholic Evidence Guild had begun by defending the Faith. She and two or three others saw quickly that defense must be secondary to exposition for the double reason that defending doctrines of which the crowd knew next to nothing was a waste of time, and that the doctrines themselves are more convincing than the arguments for them.

As experience brought the Guild speakers understanding both of the doctrines and of the listeners, she worked on a

book of Training Outlines, which went through several edi-
tions, each taking the learner deeper. She was in charge of
training the speakers — me included — both in the classroom
and on the street corner. This last was the toughest — it
meant listening outdoors to all her juniors, showing them how
they could do better, then demanding that they criticize her in
their turn. Near the end of her life she wondered if she had
not given too much of herself to this at the expense of work
more necessary. But there was no stopping her at the time; and
it is hard to think how much more other work she could have
done. She always managed to fit in one more thing.

She was one of the handful who formed the Guild rule
of never attacking another religion, never raising a laugh at
the expense of a questioner. Not that she never broke the second rule — crowds can be maddening. But she always repent-
ed. On one occasion she had been rude to a questioner. So she
began the next meeting by apologizing to him. "You'll have to
tell that in confession," he jeered. She said, "I already have."

One story often told bears repeating. A questioner had
said: "If I believed what Catholics say they believe, I wouldn't
sin. I wouldn't dare to, and anyhow I wouldn't want to. But
Catholics do sin, so clearly they don't believe." She talked of
human weakness, but he kept repeating the question, "Why
do Catholics sin?" On the fifth or sixth repetition she lost pa-
tience, leaned over him from the platform and said, "Because
they damn well choose to."

I have said that she established a relation with her
crowds. Not always, of course. There were irreconcilables by
conviction; there were people out for fun; and needless to say,

there were the drunk and disorderly. Once a very large man began swinging the whole platform so that she was in danger of being flung headlong into the crowd, he shouting the while, "I hope you've got your bloomers on." A kindly stranger saved her by offering to buy the violent one another drink.

Generally most of the listeners were on her side against the interrupters. She delighted in an old atheist on Hampstead Heath who attended the meetings regularly. One night a shrill-voiced woman kept breaking in so continually that Maisie could not be heard. The atheist, who amused himself by affecting a courtly style of utterance, said to the shrill one, "Cease twittering, wench. The damsel *shall* speak."

In Hyde Park and a score of other places in England, in New York's Times Square and down the Atlantic coast to Washington, in the Sydney Domain, she learnt to get the crowd's wavelength with incredible speed. The high peak of her skill in this came quite late in her life — she held one of the largest crowds in Times Square for an hour with quotations from Robert Browning! She had arranged them carefully in a lecture on the difficulties of *un*-believers. I would have thought it impossible. I still think it miraculous. She took absolutely for granted that she could do it.

She saw the outdoor work as a small part of "the Church's effort to get loose from the civilization that is passing away and to insert herself as a living ferment into that new civilization which is in danger of being swallowed up by paganism."

"Like Newman I feel that the presenting of Christianity, indeed of God himself, is far more vital than argument with one's fellow Christians." We should "offer the object of faith as a reality the mind can seize, not merely as the conclusion of a logical process." Thus to the argument that Christ's resurrection was only one more vegetation myth, drawn from winter with its dying and spring to follow, she would say: "If God has indeed created the world through His Word, if the coming of that Word into the world is the central event of its history, what more likely than that the seasons are modeled after the pattern of His life."

She saw what the finding of the Faith could do to converts; but saw also what converts, who have studied the Faith and made their decision about it as adults, can bring to the people they are joining: "Most of us hear the answers before we have asked the questions. It is nearly impossible to see the answer to a question you have never formulated. And without the sense of urgency that an insistent question brings, most people do not even try."

IV

Maisie had already done some writing before I met her. She was convinced that it was very bad. She asked me not to read it. I have not read it.

We had been married five or six years when she took to the pen seriously. It was with books on his father's place in the Oxford Movement, and in the Catholic Revival which flowed from it, that Wilfrid Ward had prepared himself for the writing of the life of Newman that was his masterwork. With the two books on her own parents I have already mentioned, Maisie took up the biographical tradition.

Biography, one might think, was in her blood. Yet it was not of her own motion that she set about writing *Gilbert Keith Chesterton;* Frances Chesterton asked her to.

Writing *Young Mr. Newman* was her own idea. It was a study of Newman's life up to the time of his conversion, which her father in deference to Newman's wishes had touched on lightly. The Cardinal had thought that in his books and sermons and letters he had done all that was necessary — Maisie thought this was exactly why someone else should move in: "No man knows the whole truth about himself — especially a man with a lifelong habit of self-examination! He had been too busy counting the trees to get a clear idea of the wood."

She was an unusually rapid reader — I made various efforts at calculating her speed, with results varying above and below a thousand words a minute. She read faster as she grew older. And she needed to — for she was well into her mid-seventies when she embarked on, and over eighty when she finished, her largest writing venture, the two-volume *Robert Browning and His World.*

The "embarking" was characteristic. From her teens Browning had been her favorite author. She knew hundreds of his lines by heart. But it had not occurred to her to write of him till she read a biography by a woman writer which attacked him as son, husband, friend. It infuriated her, as all injustice did. She could not be content with fury. Something had to be done. The something was the writing of nine hundred large pages, into which went the reading of six hundred books.

Her mind was quite clear as to what a biographer is supposed to be doing: "I am not writing a novel, and real life is full of open questions." She said that of her *Browning*, but it was true of them all. The novelist's characters are his own to do with as he pleases. Biographers who treat real people like that, psychoanalyzing with beaming confidence men and women they have never met, left her marveling. She could make guesses, about Browning or Newman or Chesterton, but she gives them as guesses. They explain a whole mass of problems — as when she sees in Browning an immensely complex mind but a very simple character and in Newman a lucid mind and a perplexing character — but she prefers not to assert them as facts, she simply offers them to the reader for consideration.

A third example is the movement of her mind on the question of Chesterton as mystic. Mystics, she notes, are usually ascetics. Gilbert was not ascetic in the ordinary sense, "But is there not for the thinker an asceticism of the mind, very searching, very purifying ... that sense of the pressure of thought which Newman called 'getting rid of pain by pain'; the profound depression that often follows; the exhaustion that seems like a bottomless pit. . . . Faith, thanksgiving, love, surely these far above bodily asceticism can so clear a man's eyesight that he may fittingly be called a mystic since he sees God everywhere."

God for her was not only supreme reality, but essential to all reality down to the smallest: "There is no reality without God, who has put into creation whatever reality it possesses." This had been magisterially expressed by Newman. She felt its

presence even more in Chesterton, and knew it was a presence
not to be borne lightly. Protesting against Father Vincent
McNabb's phrase "Chesterton was crucified to his thought," a
friend had said, "It was his lifelong beatitude to observe and
ponder and conclude." Maisie wondered about the beatitude:
"Intense vitality, joy in living, vigor of creative writing bring
to bear on their owners immense happiness *and* acute suffering
. . . the reaching upward and outward of the mind is at once
the keenest joy and fiercest pain."

She adds a comment which sounds like a fragment of autobiography, "The deepest pain in writing means thought
struggling to break out. But it is better than numbness."

If we take the nineteenth century as beginning with Wa-
terloo and ending with the First World War and the death of
Pius X, this was her century. With *Young Mr. Newman* she
went back to Newman's Anglican life. Her life of G.K. Chesterton was still very much in that period, though he lived
twenty years beyond it. And her *Robert Browning and His
World* was wholly within it.

Had scholarship been her first concern, she would have
stayed in it. But it never was. If her right hand found something else that urgently needed doing, it would not have occurred to her not to do it. Her contacts with people — in the
streets, in universities — convinced her, for instance, that the
general reader needed help in sorting out the mass of new
learning on the Gospels. So she wrote *They Saw His Glory,*
treating Matthew, Mark, Luke (Gospel and Acts) and John in
the light both of textual scholarship and theological thinking.
After the study of the earliest Christians as we meet them in

Acts, she found herself unable to stop. *Early Church Portrait Gallery* carries on our meeting with our ancestors in the Faith up to the year 500.

Christopher Dawson's complaint that she should have stayed with her own century, which she knew as an expert, moved her not at all. She would never say of any urgent topic, "It is not my period." Life would go on happening; things needed doing there and then; topics needed treating in books. But whether she was a professional using her scholarship or an amateur using the findings of others, there was the same thoroughness. Slapdash she could not be.

If this were a biography, Maisie's books would demand study in detail. In the context of the book I am actually writing they will be used, have in fact already been used by me, only for what they tell us of herself, or more precisely, her *self* — what the instructed heart meant in her, what part it played in the shaping of her life. "The approach to God," she wrote "is not the act of one faculty, heart or mind, but of a total human person." But the actual writing is done by the mind, and she thought long and searchingly on the distinction between Animus and Anima which meant so much to Henri Bremond, Paul Claudel and Edward Watkin. Animus is the mind we are aware of, "making its changes, working out its problems. But deep beneath, deeper even than the subconscious, lies Anima where God is still continuously creating the being He created out of nothingness, and it is at this depth that the greatest decisions of life are made."

I doubt if she ever put more of her self into any book than *The Splendor of the Rosary*. She had smiled to be told that a very learned man famed for his holiness made a habit of saying the Rosary daily in order to keep in contact with the ordinary Catholic. The Rosary Maisie saw as a superb guide to reality, not to be grown out of by anybody. Yet there was a chanciness about the book's beginning. "I had just finished writing the biography of Chesterton when John Walker of the American National Gallery of Art sent me photographs of Fra Angelico pictures, with the suggestion that they might be published as illustrations to the fifteen mysteries of the Rosary. Under the combined impact of Chesterton and Fra Angelico I wrote this book." The idea of Our Lady giving Christ back to our world was always alive in Chesterton: "Living with ideas is a wonderful thing — for most of us it is not as habitual as it was with Chesterton. But anyone of us can try it, and I have been trying it lately with the help of Chesterton, Fra Angelico and a string of beads." The whole book is practically a meditation on the instructed heart, or in her preferred phrase, "Love made wise by knowledge." Indeed it is two such meditations, for she got Caryll Houselander to write prayers in verse for each Mystery, and one instructed heart is not a carbon copy of another — Caryll, Maisie said, "fairly shouts to a neurotic world."

Reality was her continual search, its finding her contentment. In people, in ideas, in moral ideas especially, she had a faultless ear for unreality, an instant recoil. All the same she could gaze steadily at it. "There is in diabolical wickedness," she notes, "an element of the farcical."

She understood Chesterton's anger with the heartless rich, but she doubted "if he allowed enough for the degree of stupidity required to amass a fortune. He would have agreed that love of money narrowed the mind: I doubt if he fully grasped that only a mind already narrow can love money so exclusively as to possess it successfully.''

If the rich must be seen clearly, so must the saint. "To love St. Francis you need not love sanctity. If you love anything at all you will love him. There is danger in this — the danger that in the dazzle of the personality his meaning may be lost, and with his meaning his usefulness for us. . . . We miss the point if we do not see nature as only his third love — he loved God and poverty more.''

In *Saints Who Made History* she studies the quite extraordinary part played in the Church's first five centuries, as in no age since, by saints. But her realism never wanes before the holiest of them. Thus she sees running through Eastern Christianity a shrinking from the "Word made flesh," a "tendency to see God as infinitely distant, unknowable, unapproachable by men." She goes on: "We see something of the same feeling even in orthodox Eastern mystics, such as the exquisite poet Ephrem of Syria. 'Search out the sea,' he says, 'but search not the Lord of the sea.' Loving the Faith as a hidden mystery, he attacked those who tried 'to see the air, to handle the light.' But," she adds, " 'We *have* handled,' says St. John; and the Light Himself told Thomas to handle Him, told us all to eat Him that we might have life.''

She summarizes a whole line of spirituality as "one bodiless spirit trying to lead another to the God who had not created them bodiless.''

V

Rare are the intellectuals who have devoted so much time and labor as she to coping with men's material needs. She knew the troubled Jesuit Father Tyrrell, and it was from her that I heard his bitter gibe about Catholic charity — that when the Church finds people in the gutter she blesses the gutter. This was to ignore such an ocean of aid to the needy as no other institution can approach. Epigrams, of course, always get their effect by leaving out too much, and there was enough official heartlessness to account for this one. But nobody, I fancy, would have thought of saying it, even as an epigram, about Maisie — so deeply, irrevocably, was she immersed in working to meet human needs. It was not in her to pass by on the other side.

There was homelessness, for instance. "I think of a priest who gave a home for months in his presbytery to a homeless colored family. One baby was born in this marvelous Bethlehem." From the beginning of our married life she was helping friends to buy homes, advancing money for down payments. In the depression of the early thirties she bought a farm in Sussex, on which four town boys sent by a Catholic land association were to be trained as farmers — she paying all the expenses, they to take any profits; but there was too much the men behind the scheme did not know: in a couple of years it folded.

But she was not through with farming. After the Second World War thousands of Polish soldiers were living in encampments in England: she bought another farm and put one of them to manage it. After an uncertain beginning this one worked out well.

The farms we may think of as a rehearsal for the Catholic Housing Aid Society, which she founded with Molly Walsh — whose own heart deserves a separate study. Maisie was sixty-six when she came to realize the desperate meaning of the four million houses destroyed by the bombing. There is no space here for a detailed description of the planning and running of the Association. She gave her own money, squeezed money out of her friends, persuaded Catholic lawyers to do conveyancing work free. My own memory is of homeless families ringing our doorbell at 2 A.M. In the first year's balance sheet, the overhead expenses came to something like five pounds, with twelve families housed; next year the expenses had shot up to twelve pounds, with thirty families housed. Then came the collaboration with Father Eamonn Casey, on loan from Ireland and now Bishop of Galway, and the development of the Housing Association. For the second time I quote him: "She was a woman of iron will and strict observance, and yet could respond with gentleness and understanding to human need and frailty in others. She was a woman whose utter trust and confidence in others who worked with her was partly the secret of her inspiration. . . . The problems of the most insignificant individual became her problems, and the organization had to look smart when she got after them."

She was seventy-five when she retired from the Housing Association, leaving it in excellent health and spirits: at the time of her death eleven years later, it reported 2,000 families housed in London alone, with other centers all over England.

Of housing and much beside she tells the story in her autobiography, *Unfinished Business.* The "much beside" I merely glance at. While our children were growing up, her duty to them placed a solid limit to work outside the home: once they were married the sky was the limit. She was much in France, seeing and discussing with Priest-Workmen in Paris and in Marseille (she wrote small books on both). She was profoundly interested in Dorothy Day and the Catholic Worker movement in America. The Black Panther movement among Negroes she followed closely, feeling deep in herself how, if she had been black, the movement would have drawn her to it. In Australia's Northern Territory she met Aborigines in real life, having known them and found her imagination gripped by them in the detective stories of Arthur Upfield.

Among all the problems of which she tells in *Unfinished Business,* two took a special hold on her heart. One was the work founded in Australia by Father Con Keogh to do for neurotics what Alcoholics Anonymous had done for the drink-soaked in America. The other was the plight of the wives and children of imprisoned Conscientious Objectors to the Vietnam War. From every meeting with them she came home emotion-drained.

To any of the matters I have listed in these two paragraphs she would gladly have given herself wholly, but there remained the two prior commitments — the offering of Christ's gifts to the millions who were starving for want of them, and the housing of the homeless.

For a woman of seventy-five, the title *Unfinished Business* sounds like a challenge to whatever gods there be. It was simply her version of a Kipling line that she loved — "There's no discharge from the war." The eleven years that followed were fantastically filled with two new labors. There was her vast toil on the Robert Browning books, and there was the aid she gave to priests putting untouchables on their own land in India — Father Van der Valk in Andra Pradesh, northwest of Madras, and Father Zucol in Kerala.

To raise money she tried everything. She told of the work to anyone she could persuade to listen, getting 1,500 pounds from a man she met (for the first time) at dinner in a friend's house; she wrote and lectured; she persuaded priests to let her preach and take a collection at Mass — on one glorious occasion there was a check for $1,000 in the plate.

She once said, "If only I had four times as much energy." I started to say, "You'd need four husbands to help you cope." I never finished the sentence, as I realized how little she had ever called on me to help in her countless labors. I was reminded of it when I went with her to Andra Pradesh, where the whole town, Catholic and Hindu alike, had come to own cooperatively a huge and growing area of land made productive. There were three nights of celebrations with bonfires and dances and chanting. She was feted almost as a cult goddess, I receiving the respect due to the goddess's consort. Which I was delighted to be.

Of the Browning book and India and much else she tells in *To and Fro on the Earth*. The title she took from the opening of the Book of Job: "The Lord said to Satan, 'Whence have you come?' Satan answered, 'From going to and fro on the earth and from walking up and down on it.' And the Lord

said to Satan, 'Have you considered my servant Job . . .?' "
Maisie's comment: "The earth of course is not Satan's. I have
gone to and fro on it myself and have walked up and down on
it — and I have considered Job."

From this book, one last quotation: "Creation is at work
everywhere, on a large scale occasionally, but more signifi-
cantly in small-scale achievements by the hundred, by the
thousand. All over the world I have found small groups who
are building a new world in the shell of the one crumbling
around us."

The
Heart
in Scripture

CHAPTER TWO

The Heart in Scripture *

I

The phrase on which I have been asked to speak, *cor ad cor*, I first met in the motto John Henry Newman chose for his arms as Cardinal, *Cor ad cor loquitur*, "Heart speaks to heart." From the *Life* written by my wife's father, Wilfrid Ward, we learn that Newman thought it was a quotation — perhaps from the Vulgate, perhaps from the *Imitation of Christ*. He wondered if perhaps it should be *cor cordi*. He asked one of the Fathers of the Oratory to track it down for him. In fact he had himself used the phrase — as *cor cordi loquitur* — a quarter century before. In a paper on University Preaching he had given it as part of a longer Latin quotation from St. Francis de Sales: "Though the words issue from the mouth, the heart speaks to the heart, the tongue beats only on the ears." Had Newman forgotten that he had found it in St. Francis, or was he wondering where St. Francis got it? Either way, as *cor ad cor* it seems to be Newman's own.

What did it mean to him? Whose are the two hearts,

(With some additions and subtractions this is a paper read at Paray-le-Monial on the three-hundredth anniversary of the Revelations to Saint Margaret Mary.)

that their discourse was of such importance to him that he should thus choose it in that moment of the crowning by the Church of his lifework? Not his own heart and Cardinal Manning's, I think, still less his own and Pius IX's. Given that Newman and Manning wrote so glowingly of the Sacred Heart and Pius extended the feast to the Universal Church, there is perhaps a warning for us in the discovery that Newman's heart was barely on speaking terms with either of theirs.

We tend to assume that the two hearts are man's and God's; and this is the profoundest truth of God's fatherhood. But as St. Francis used the words and Newman quoted them, the two hearts are the heart of the preacher and the heart of the hearer. Both men are making a particular application to preaching of a truth concerning all human communication — what is not *cor ad cor* is a mere beating of the ears.

But you certainly have not asked me here to talk of Newman's general theories on preaching. We are met at Paray-le-Monial to rejoice in the showings of the Sacred Heart to St. Margaret Mary. Newman will not mind my applying his phrase primarily to preaching on the Sacred Heart of Jesus. And you, I hope, will not mind a layman speaking to you about preaching. My wife and I have had forty-eight years of teaching the Faith at thousands of meetings under the open skies of England and America and Australia — to believers, half-believers, unbelievers, who challenged us to justify every word we used.

What is the Heart that St. Margaret Mary and we are honoring? In *The Glories of the Sacred Heart of Jesus* Cardinal Manning states it for us, ". . . the heart of flesh, taken from the substance of his Mother, united with the eternal charity and sanctity of God." One early enthusiast had written that "as the soul sees through the eyes, so it loves through the heart"; Cardinal Lambertini — who as Benedict XIV was to state the devotion to the Sacred Heart so accurately — censured this as bad physiology. But if we no longer think of the heart of flesh as seat or source of our emotions, we still know it as uniquely responsive to them.

In Gerard Manley Hopkins's words, the heart is not the source of our emotions but their register — "the one organ which most strongly and of its own accord sympathizes with and expresses in itself what goes on in the soul . . . the beating of the heart is the truth of nature." In love the heart does beat faster as the liver does not. The cynic may point out that this gives the heart an undeserved priority as a register of love: after all, emotion or no emotion, the heart's *raison d'être* is to beat; how else (the Scripture writers did not know about that) could the blood circulate? It remains that men of our world have tended to see the heart as the symbol of love.

Newman saw the Sacred Heart so. We have his prayer: "Make my heart beat with Thy heart: purify it of all that is earthly, proud and sensual, hard and cruel, of all perversity, disorder, deadness." He knew the Scriptures as few men have known them, and from end to end of Scripture the heart is indeed associated with love, but with a great deal besides. In the Old Testament much that we link with spirit is credited to the heart — knowledge, wisdom, thought, decisions, hardness, wilfulness, repentance. "Rend your hearts and not your garments," says Joel (2:13); Deuteronomy has the same idea: "Circumcise the foreskin of your heart" (10:16). In the moment of his stoning, Stephen could accuse his slayers: "Stiff-necked people, uncircumcised in heart and ears" (Acts 7:51). Ezekiel (36:26) tells of God's saying, "A new heart I will give you, a new spirit I will put within you; I will take out of your flesh the heart of stone and give you a heart of flesh"; hard to think that this was not in Robert Burns' memory when he said of promiscuous sex, "It hardens all within and petrifies the feeling."

Scripture does not use the psychological terms Christians have grown used to — with thinking and knowledge in the mind or intellect, for instance, love and decision in the will. Heart covers all that. Where the Greeks taught us to say "Know thyself," Psalm 4 has it, "Commune with your own heart." "To steal one's heart" has a highly sentimental value with us; in Genesis 31 it means "to deceive." "Lacking heart" with us means either cruelty or failure of nerve; in Proverbs it means "stupid" — the examples given are committing adultery and visiting a prostitute!

Thinking is done with the heart. I cannot recall an instance of Scripture linking thought with the head; "brain" it never uses at all. And though it does link love with the heart, it is usually in relation to the love God offers it, less often to man's own loving. Less often, indeed, but once supremely: "You shall love the Lord your God, with your whole heart and soul and strength." From this, as Christ tells us, it follows that we must love our neighbor as we love ourself. "On these two depend the law and the prophets," the whole of life now and life everlastingly.

One of the most surprising episodes in Scripture is told in chapter 20 of Genesis. If you are making any study at all of God and the human heart, it is essential reading. Arrived in the territory of Abimelech, Abraham said that his wife Sarah was his sister and told her to say the same — for fear that the king would kill him and take Sarah. (This deception Abraham had already practiced on Pharaoh.) So Abimelech (who had a wife) took Sarah. God threatened him with the punishment he had deserved for taking Abraham's wife. Abimelech's answer was that both of them had said she was his sister, and he pleaded, "In the integrity of my heart and the innocence of my hands I have done this." And God accepted his plea for forgiveness: "I know you have done this in the integrity of your heart." This is Scripture's first use of "integrity." There are later uses which startle us less.

Over the centuries men's "understanding" of the will of God has of course varied enormously, as has their idea of God Himself. It would not be possible here to record the variations. But it is the heart itself we are considering: its health depends on how it copes with whatever of reality it has come to see, whether by divine revelation or by man's meditation on his own experience. It is hard to think of any human reaction, good or bad, that Scripture does not see in man's heart: but most of all it sees the emotions — sorrow, joy, discouragement, a heart heavy or merry, or both together, "sad even in laughter," trembling, broken, gladdened by wine, lusting after a woman. All these are involved with love or the refusal of love, and Newman saw the Sacred Heart as "the instrument or organ of Christ's love, beating for us, yearning over us."

The words "spirit" and "heart" are in both Testaments, and they seem to be almost interchangeable, as in the Ezekiel verse just quoted. In both, spirit is used for God *and* man, heart mainly for man. Yet not exclusively; we meet God's heart too. Very early in Genesis (6:5-6) we read that "God saw that the wickedness of man was great on the earth and that every imagination of the thoughts of his heart was only evil continually." Because of the multitudinous evil in men, He "was sorry he had made man, and it grieved him to his heart." It is the first time God's heart and man's are mentioned together.

It is not the last. King David said to God, "According to your own heart you have wrought all this greatness" (2 Samuel 7:21). And Samuel had already spoken of David as a man after God's own heart (1 Samuel 13:14). None of this is to be written off as a primitive way of speaking which men will outgrow; a thousand years after David, Paul had not outgrown it. In the synagogue of Antioch in Pisidia he could tell of God as saying, "I have found in David, the son of Jesse, a man after my own heart . . ." (Acts 13:22). Knowing David, we may have found this surprising on Paul's lips. To us less spectacular sinners there is some reassurance in the discovery that God's judgments are not always ours: as with Pharaoh and Abimelech, Scripture shows Him making allowances! There is more reassurance still in the very rich young man Jesus loved who went away sorrowful because he could not give up his wealth (Luke 18:23). Jesus, it is clear, loves sinners. He wants us to stop sinning, he helps us to stop, but he does not withhold his love till we *have* stopped.

Man is made in God's image; of what in God does Scripture see the human heart as the image? The whole life. With every difference of modality, one life embraces God and God-man, and man. The conversation my heart is trying to have with yours at this moment draws what poor quality it has from such conversation as you and I have had with the heart of the Savior; His conversation with us draws its richness from the eternal interflow of love and life between Father and Son from which proceeds the Holy Spirit.

That last sentence is so easy to say. You have doubtless heard or said it often enough from your pulpits, as I have from my platforms. But if we pause to think of its immensity, I wonder if we hear what we are saying.

II

What I shall say next concerns priests, as men whose function is to mediate doctrine and devotion: but in essence it applies to all Christians who accept the duty of sharing their knowledge of Christ with those who lack a knowledge so life-giving.

When I was young, most of the sermons I heard on the Sacred Heart conveyed nothing save that the preacher was excited by it: if he was a famous preacher he seemed to be on fire with it. But he did not make it clear to us what it was that excited or inflamed him. If the sermon was a success, the congregation was all vibrant; but it was vibrating not to the Heart of Jesus but solely to the preacher's vibrations. Myself, I did not vibrate. Invariably I found it embarrassing and wished he would stop.

With this we are at the last word of Newman's motto — *loquitur*, "speaks." Heart must speak to heart — but not only or mainly by heartbeats. There must be words, reality stated to the limit of our ability, faith made luminous by doctrine, as Vatican II phrases it. Throughout the Christian world today there is an impatience with doctrinal statements: men feel them shallow: the infinite, they remind us, cannot be conveyed in words or even contained in words; what really matters is the impact revelation makes upon us. But without clear statement, impact is of less value; we do not know what has hit us. The statements made by Scripture or the Teaching Church are indeed shallower than God, but they are not shallower than we, and by them we can move out of the shallows. As Newman says in his *University Sermons,* "Nothing would indicate a more shallow philosophy than to say that faith ought to be distinguished from dogmatic statements." "*Loquitur*" was not the word he would have chosen for the downgrading of words.

Transfer this contrast between statement and impact to the pulpit. Words can of course be used to batter the will to acceptance and stimulate the emotions to hysteria: in too many sermons they have been used like that. It is the way of quick results, but there is no permanence in them; however eloquent the preacher, a time must come when eloquence and preacher alike will be no more than a fragrant memory. But words employed to bring light to the mind can build the truth firmly into the mind's substance, whence it will have its genuine effect on will and imagination and emotions, in fact upon the whole inner life, which for Scripture is the heart's function.

Fervent sermons about the Sacred Heart to people who have only a sketchy half-remembered idea of the Christ of the Gospels, people to whom Incarnation and Trinity are formulas which have never opened up their reality, come close to those "idle words" for every one of which Our Lord says men will have to render an account at the Judgment (Matthew 12:36). The reason given for that sort of preaching was that the average man was incapable of understanding the great dogmas. The experience of the street-corner speakers of the Catholic Evidence Guild showed the falsity of this underrating of the ordinary man's intellect. Our method was for each speaker to lecture for fifteen or twenty minutes, then take questions for the rest of the hour. In London's Hyde Park we talked every night in the week and for eight hours on Sunday. In the question period the crowds pressed us against the furthest limits of our knowledge in every area of Revelation. I find it hard to think of any problem raised by heretics in nineteen hundred years that our questioners have not hurled at us, or mocked us with. There was no danger of our talking down to them: our whole effort was to keep up with them; they forced us to realize that we could not meet their depths with our shallows. In our first years we avoided the doctrine of the Trinity, convinced that we could not utter it adequately, and that our crowds would not respond to it at all. At last we had to face the fact that if we avoided speaking of Father, Son and Holy Spirit we were not offering our hearers the God of Jesus Christ but only the God of Unitarians and Mohammedans.

In almost as much fear and trembling as St. Paul thinks necessary for the working out of our salvation, we began to teach what the Church had to give us on the Trinity; and we made the discovery that the crowds were fascinated by it. About this we could not be wrong, because we were speaking to non-captive audiences: if they were not interested they would walk away and leave us talking to ourselves, delivering not a speech but a soliloquy. Pause upon this. Nothing develops a speaker so much as having his hearers leave him. I would not trust anyone with a captive audience until he had proved he could hold one that was free to go away. The speaker who had used his mind on Father, Son and Holy Spirit — not figures of speech but the doctrine itself — was certain of an audience.

This was indeed part of a larger lesson we learnt about all our teaching. One teaches, not by offering the audience a truth accurately stated, but by effecting a union of minds, or as Scripture would say, hearts — the speaker's, the listener's. As a result of this union a truth living in the one heart may become a truth living in the other. As in bodily union, both parties must be in action: as in bodily union, love should be the living element. In the conveyance of the truths of revelation, *cor ad cor loquitur* is the only effective formula, whether one person is speaking to many from a platform or one is talking to another chance-met in train or plane.

Love demands that we study the heart and mind of those we must teach. We must know the atmosphere they breathe, the atmosphere of the world in which they (and we of course) must live — its way of thinking, its values, its vocabulary —

above all its vocabulary! I remember a seminarian saying to a crowd on Hampstead Heath, "God is pure act, there is no potentiality in God"; they thought he was saying that God is virtuous but impotent.

III

Apply all this to the teaching of the Sacred Heart. The whole point of the doctrine is God's love channeled to men in the heart which the Second Person made his own. But God's love seems to be fading out of general Christian awareness. Christ is still allowed to have loved men, but God is above all that! Some of Christianity's most widely known spokesmen — Catholics included — seem to have arrived non-mystically at the impersonal, unfeeling Absolute of so much Eastern mysticism. Some, of course, have been reading Plotinus, but without Augustine's ability to take what he needed from Plotinus and then sweat him out of his system.

The mystic, Shankara or Plotinus or Eckhart or St. John of the Cross, has made contact with the root of his own being, the ultimate point, one assumes, at which nothingness is made into something by Omnipotence; I find myself wondering if some of them at least were not confronting only the nothingness and mistaking it for the Absolute (which of course, in one direction, nothingness is!). However that may be, there was a sense of a godhead beyond God, featureless, in the infinite stillness of utterly undifferentiated oneness, not knowing individuals in any sense of knowing known to us, not loving them therefore.

I get the impression that for many, even Christian, mystics the Trinity is merely the face shown to us by the Absolute, which has no face. One meets an intoxication with the nothingness out of which our Creator drew us, a *nostalgie du rien.* Some of today's most articulate Christians have reached a god equally featureless, not by the way of mystical experience but by the way of inertia (which may well be a magnetism of nothingness). God is still named with reverence, but not much adverted to, not seen as having any stateable function, a sort of non-luminous cloud on the religious mind's horizon.

Alike against the mystics of the Impersonal and the preachers of the impersonal stands the God of both Testaments. Here we face a mystery which looks like sheer contradiction: we must use our minds upon it; we must help our hearers to cope with it.

Philosophy shows us God as infinite and immutable, so that creatures cannot affect Him. Scripture shows us God as affected by what creatures do. Metaphysically it is unthinkable that the Absolute should react to, be affected by, beings He has made of naught; yet Scripture presents God as "affected," as "reacting," with love or pity or rage, with reward or punishment — pitying as a father pities his children, loving Israel with a mother's love, pleading for men's love in return. In *God and the Human Mind* I wrote: "Both statements, God concerned with us and God unconcerned, are colliding with the limits of human language and human thought in the attempt to utter a truth by us unutterable. Each is at once a superb effort and an inevitable failure to utter the whole of reality, which is beyond our vision. To hold the one view would

seem to put care and sorrow into God, to make the Almighty
vulnerable to us; but to hold the other gives a monster god to
whom it is a matter of indifference whether we suffer or don't
suffer, sin or don't sin. Compassion as men experience it,
transferred to God, would seem to connote a defect in infinite
beatitude; but indifference would seem to connote a worse
kind of defect still, a defect in love."

Philosophy is the work of men seeking an ultimate explanation of the universe. Revelation is the work of God, who *is*
the ultimate explanation of the universe seeking to be known
by men. For believers, Revelation has God's guarantee of its
truth; philosophy has no guarantee at all — only the hearers'
conviction that its findings satisfy some need or awareness in
themselves. For a believer there is no question which holds the
priority.

The words "absolute" and "infinite," in which the
seeming contradiction rests, are not in Scripture. Greek philosophy arrived at them, and in their naked meaning — God's
limitless fullness of being, God wholly self-existent, dependent
for being and action on no other — and Christian theologians
have found them lifegiving. But what infinity and absolute-
ness *are in themselves*, what consequences (so to speak) flow
from them, only one who possesses them can know. The rest is
speculation — logic, insight, flashes in the dark. The Greeks
did speculate, brilliantly and with total assurance. Many
Christian thinkers have treated their speculating as revelation.
Aristotle's concept of God as Pure Act, with whatever it owed
to Indian philosophers and mystics, is a high point of human
philosophy. But if it keeps us from seeing, or has us explaining

away, the God who is Christ's Father and ours, then Aristotle has served us badly. And there is no question that one result of that long tradition of an impersonal Absolute is that some of our thinkers seem to be warning us of God's unsuitability for the union with us that He so clearly and continuously wants, which in its fullness He sets as the goal of man's existence.

Perhaps that is why Pascal preferred the God of Abraham, Isaac and Jacob. So did Christ. He reminded the Sadducees that the God of the three patriarchs was a God not of the dead but of the living. And He shows God as knowing, hearing, listening, caring, loving, giving himself, withdrawing himself: God clothes the grasses of the field; no sparrow falls without God seeing. The Old Testament had shown God as wanting man's trust, wanting men to open their hearts to his in prayer, loving men and wanting their love. Christ carries us one stage deeper, leaving us in no doubt that God wants to be known by us: "No one knows the Father but the Son and him to whom the Son shall reveal him." He leaves us no doubt either that God wants us in the closest union with Himself. "I am in my Father," He says at the Last Supper (John 14:20), "and you in me, and I in you." This not in some future life but here and now, though its fullest flowering is to be in heaven.

On the Cross His heart spoke: "Father forgive them, for they know not what they do" (Luke 23:34). This cannot by any theological refinement be reconciled with an infinite indifference, or with the view that what man does makes no difference. There is a reality in the Absolute which forgives men because of their ignorance, which acts differently according to whether men do or do not realize the meaning of their own acts, which can be asked in prayer to do thus or thus.

What this reality is we do not know. But it is not less real because there is no adequate human utterance for it. God thought it better that we should have it thus rather than not at all. There *is* something within the changeless, infinite, absolute God which, reduced to words we can hear, is mercy or sorrow or anger — heart, in fact — which yet leaves Him changeless, infinite, absolute. What it is we cannot know (save in a mirror) until we see Him face to face.

IV

From the world in which so many Christians must live, God is almost wholly absent. The religious leaders they meet in books and newspapers see Him as beyond personality; those who see Him as the fullness of personality are simply not heard often enough because they stay silent. So the ordinary Christian to whom God is little more than a name will tend in the practical running of his life not to think of Him at all. Christ's first commandment is left in a void — how love a being to whom no function is attached? So their energy is switched wholly to Christ's second commandment, "Love your neighbor." But the first commandment is the very lifeblood of the second. Only God can help us to live with, and love, our neighbors. Indeed loving God sounds easier than loving many of the people we actually meet. The preacher must try to help his hearers to a living awareness of Christ's God. It is from the disciple Jesus loved that we get the actual phrase, "God is love" — (I John 4:8,16) not much doubt where *he* got it.

Newman, reminded by St. Francis de Sales, reminds us that there must be a union of hearts if a truth living in one is to become a truth living in another. However much the teacher may know about the hearts of his hearers and the pressure they are under, he will profit them nothing unless the truth he wishes to convey is alive in himself. When his topic is the Sacred Heart, what must its aliveness in himself mean?

The Gospels he must know intimately, of course. I do not mean the rags and tatters that remain after the latest critic has done his worst. I mean Matthew, Mark, Luke and John as men have seen the face of Christ in them through all the centuries. He may decide for new interpretations, but only if he knows what is actually there. The critics have plenty to teach him, but only if he has his own personal intimacy with Jesus of Nazareth; for it is still the same face, and what matters for our present purpose, it is still the same heart. The general picture of the kind of man Jesus of Nazareth was — His values and priorities, the light He flashes into the heart of man — emerges little changed. And these things matter vitally if we are to teach people about the Sacred Heart.

His heart, indeed, is the one thing most people are sure about. But it is a heart ill-comprehended, all sugar and sweetness, seen so because they do not know the Jesus of the public life. For most of us the light falls upon Him twice — in Bethlehem and in the Passion, largely perhaps because the Creed goes straight from "born of the Virgin Mary" to "suffered under Pontius Pilate," and the Rosary has nothing between the Finding in the Temple and the Agony in the Garden. The Nativity and the Passion are insufficient for full knowledge of Jesus — the Nativity because one baby looks much like another, the Passion because, with His victimhood come to its climax, He was different. Only in the public life we meet what may be called His everyday self.

It is a self notably unsentimental. He is not given to expressing His love in words. We are told — not by Himself — of a handful of people He loved. There were the Apostles (whom He loved "to the end"), the rich young man (whose great possessions came between him and Jesus), the family at Bethany, the unnamed disciple "whom Jesus loved." He could be harsh even to His friends — "foolish" and "slow of heart," He called the two disciples at Emmaus. And He could rage against God's enemies. To the chief priests and the elders He said that "the tax gougers and prostitutes shall go into the kingdom of God before you" — those words must have helped to ensure His crucifixion.

With this very complex Jesus each must make his own intimacy. He is not to be studied merely as a piece in the diagram of redemption, an automaton walking majestically the way planned for Him by His heavenly Father, with no individual reactions of His own till Gethsemani, when He startles us with His "not my will but yours." Even Catholics who know their theology reasonably well can fail to see how markedly individual He was.

What God the Son assumed was not simply human nature, but that particular human nature. He became not man in the abstract, but that man, the son of that mother. With ancestors forty generations back in the direct line to David (and how many thousands of generations beyond David to mankind's beginning!), He had his own genes and chromosomes. Some things therefore came easily to Him, some less easily; He had His own likes and dislikes. He had a heart like ours; otherwise He could not have been tested in all things as we are. He had a will like ours: which of us has not said, or found it all but impossible to say, "Not my will but Yours"? What conflicts His will might have had to overcome we can know only if He tells us — and of His own inner life He tells us so little. What He does tell us is at once precious and tantalizing. "There is a baptism with which I must be baptized, and how am I constrained till it be accomplished" (Luke 12:50). The waiting for the Passion and Death, the baptism in His blood, was a strain He found it hard to live with; yet when it was upon Him His first cry was, "Let this cup pass from me."

A symbol exists in the response it evokes. In a given man, or in a whole generation, the heart used symbolically may produce no illumination, no stirring at all. But the reality symbolized does not depend on the symbol. The Sacred Heart of Jesus was not in itself a metaphor or symbol: His heart was wholly real and wholly sacred, as real and sacred as the humanity the Son had made His own. In the Sacred Heart Devotion it is a symbol. Of what? Of His love, primarily, for to Him love was primary. In two texts from the Old Testament, one from Deuteronomy and one from Leviticus, He gave love for God and love for man as the vitalizing principles of the Law and the Prophets. A refusal of love is a failure in life; a final refusal means failure eternally. It is notable that He attaches eternal loss almost wholly to our failure to love our fellow men, possibly on the principle stated by John in his first Epistle — if we don't love our neighbor whom we see, how shall we love God whom we don't see?

V

Love being of such literally vital importance, a matter of eternal life and death, we had better clarify our minds about it. It would be catastrophic to be wrong about our own love. It is strange that Jesus does not tell us what love is but only what love does, which is not quite the same thing. "Greater love has no man than that he lay down his life for his friends" (John 15:13). This rates death for a friend as love's highest gift: all the same, the dying is not the love. Paul admonishes that "if I give my body to be burnt and have not love it avails me nothing" (I Corinthians 13:3). So one might die without love. All Our Lord is saying is that willingness to die is the supreme proof of love — provided love is there, as Paul reminds us. The level of love in ourselves we must judge by looking at all the tests of love Jesus gives.

They fall mainly under two headings — we must give, and we must forgive. Both are frightening if we take them seriously; it is hard to know which — giving or forgiving — we find more costly.

There is no sin Our Lord attacks more frequently, none He finds more heartless, than love of money. If we do not feed the hungry, give drink to the thirsty, clothe the naked, then it is Himself we are refusing, and the penalty is everlasting fire (Matthew 25:31-46). We have read the passage, or heard it read, a hundred times. It is a perfect example of the habit most of us have of reading Scripture in a state of pious coma. We glide so easily over the words, "neither did you do it to me"; we hardly notice "Depart from me"; the "everlasting fire" could have no relevance to nice people like us. And we weigh carefully how much of our comfortable surplus we can spare for the world's misery.

How is Jesus to make us listen? A camel, he tells us, gets through the eye of a needle more easily than a rich man into the kingdom of heaven. The disciples at last were stirred from their coma — did Jesus really mean that salvation was not possible for the rich? "To man," Jesus answered, "it is impossible; but to God all things are possible" — even the salvation of the rich! Yet who of us would not wish to be rich! Giving, then, is one test of love; most of us do not get a high mark. Forgiving is another; is our mark any better? I remember an excited member of an outdoor crowd shouting, "You must forgive unto seventy times seven and not once more, saith the Lord!" But what Jesus was telling us was that we must forgive without limit. In the Sermon on the Mount He says, "If you do not forgive others, your heavenly Father will not forgive you" (Matthew 6:14). Each of us, unless he "forgives his brother from his heart," will be treated like the man to whom mercy has been shown and who proceeds to act mercilessly (Matthew 18:35). Do we hear our Lord saying this? Do we even hear ourselves, every time we say the Our Father, making God's forgiveness for us dependent on our forgiving others?

VI

I have concentrated on the heart of Jesus as an organ of love. But for Jesus Himself, as throughout Scripture, the heart is the source of the whole of man's inner life. Paul, whose own heart speaks so richly of Christ's heart, could tell the Corinthians (1.2:16) that "we have the *mind* of Christ" — in Greek, *nous*; that in Christ which did the knowing, the seeing. There has been a tendency in writers and preachers to split Christ down the middle, so to speak — to base all on the heart and let the mind take its chance. But He is one Christ. It would be a kind of blindness to try to love as Christ loved without seeing the reality Christ saw.

The teacher must be living mentally in the same universe as Christ, must be helping his hearers to live in it. It is not enough merely to know about it, he and they must be living in it: the knowledge of reality as Christ saw it must not be only in the mind's files, available for reference; it must be in the mind's landscape. What did Christ *see?* A thousand things, of course, but two principally, a greater and a less great. We do not find either easy to keep constantly in sight. The less is the transience of our earthly life. If eye or hand or foot lead us into sin we must pluck out eye, cut off and cast from us hand or foot — better to enter life with one of each than to be cast complete with two into the fire that does not die. This makes life on earth not less important but more: in a sense deeper than Keats knew, it is "The vale of Soul-making." Here on earth we are fashioning the self which for bliss or woe is to be ours everlastingly.

But the weightiest thing that Christ *saw*, and therefore we must see, is God everywhere present, our relation to Him the essence of our identity: "Whoever does the will of my Father is my brother and sister and mother" (Mark 3:35). So Christ's God is not the impersonal absolute, whether of the mystic or the metaphysician: He has a will for us. His will is nourishment: "My food is to do the will of him who sent me . . ." (John 4:34). And it is decisive. But the decision is ours, not God's. He will not refuse us, but we can refuse Him. Love is the one gift the weakest can refuse omnipotence.

But at a moment when God is not much adverted to, how real can be our awareness of God's love? A shift of emphasis in our understanding of the Sacrifice of the Mass would help. Sexual union is essentially a union in love, a fact hidden from many a devout Catholic by St. Paul's speaking of it (I Corinthians 7:3) as "rendering the debitum," paying the debt. The Mass too, which is Calvary as Christ now offers it to His heavenly Father, is essentially a union in love; but this is hidden for many by the emphasis on obligation — just one more debitum to be rendered!

In offering Mass we are in the closest union with the heart of Christ. But what of God to whom we join with Christ in making the offering? Christ has a heart; so have we. Has God? We must avoid what looks like an easy way out — the fact that by Christ's union with the Father and the Spirit, there is at least a heart in the Godhead, if only a human heart. Indeed no mere humanitarian ever dreamed of humanity raised to so high a level. Yet it is not love's summit, not the highest love by which we humans can be vitalized. I do not exaggerate in saying that love in the Godhead for many Catholics is represented only by the Sacred Heart of Christ — a notion Christ Himself could view only with horror. Compared with ours the love of His human heart is a furnace, but it is a candle flame compared to the furnace of divine love, its supreme value being that it was lit from that furnace. He knew Himself as the way, not the goal. His mission was to bring the Spirit to us, bring us to the Father. It is *the love with which the Father loved Him* that He prays may be in His followers.

We may not find it easy to see it so, to feel it so. The man Christ Jesus is under our gaze as the Father is not, sharing our experiences as the Father cannot. We can but hope, as Christ and His heart become more real to us, that His God and ours, His Father and ours, may in the same measure become more real to us. We must grow into seeing God not as a problem to be solved, or even as a solution to be admired, but as a reality to be contemplated, conversed with, loved and possessed, even here on earth, as it was by Christ who is our Brother.

The
Heart
in Us

CHAPTER THREE

The Heart in Us

I

Between the people of Scripture and the people that we meet — the people in fact that we are — the resemblance can be unnerving. Nineteen hundred years of Christianity seem to have made so little difference.

At their high point, of course, the children of Israel had a vast amount from God — His creation of the world and man, His majesty, His love for them, the prophets He sent them. But their high point they reached only gradually in the fifteen centuries or so between Abraham and Gamaliel. Yet from the very beginning we can see ourselves — to say nothing of our friends — in some of the best of them and some of the worst.

We meet Abraham, lying to save his life from Pharoah and Abimelech (they were in our last chapter); Rachel, who fooled Isaac and mourned for her children; Laban, who fooled Jacob and spared his life; David, treating Bathsheba's husband so foully and mourning for slain Absalom. One could put all the Old Testament names into a hat and draw, with the high probability of drawing a name of someone we could match at once.

And this is true not only of the people we meet in Scripture. Wherever we meet man — highly developed or utterly primitive — we know him for a fellow creature, his "heart" recognizably human. That heart is the raw material on which all religions and all civilizations have to work. Some do it better than others: we know much of how Israel did it; we know how the Church does it — with rebirth into Christ and doctrine and sacrament. But for all of them the work has to start on each of their members at birth, finding the same kind of core-resistance to the control of the self which all call for — curious that the word "unselfishness" is not in Scripture. The hearts of ourselves and our long-dead spiritual ancestors seem almost interchangeable. Underneath what religion and the experience of living have done to correct and develop them, their values are much like ours. And in any study of the heart, value is a master-word.

As a verb and as a noun, it has two quite different meanings; a lot of tragedy lies in their difference. The verb first: we value what we think worth having, admire in others, wish we ourselves had. The objects we value vary immeasurably. That people should pay vast sums for postage stamps, bits of colored paper, has always been beyond my understanding. I remember thinking how much more comprehensible to collect diamonds — until I met a diamond merchant who put all his profits into buying stamps: he assured me that they had never been known to fall in value (money value, that is). But this of course was merely the interest of the dealer; he wanted to make money. What still puzzles me is the genuine collector, who values stamps — or diamonds — for themselves.

What individuals value varies in value right down to the utterly valueless. Which brings us to the noun: real value, things valuable in themselves even if no one values them — or even knows about them (like vitamin B or insulin before they were discovered). Such things have real value, because of their relation to reality: they are valued by us according to our knowledge of reality. In the bodily order this test goes without question; bodily health results from knowing the laws of reality and living by them. So, but less obviously, does mental health. So, but to many not obviously at all, does moral health. We are in a real world. To be out of harmony with it in any area of our life must damage us.

Knowing the laws *and living by them.* Our health depends, alas, not only on how much of reality and its laws the intellect sees: there is the will, the second partner in Scripture's "heart." It decides what we choose to do in each situation as the intellect shows it. If only it could be counted on to make its choice of actions in the light of reality as intellect sees it! But the will's tendency — controlled in some more than in others but in few wholly — is to clutch at what we want and evade what we dislike. It is even more subject than the intellect to imagination and emotions.

Though one wonders . . . There is what Alexander Pope calls the "insupportable fatigue of thought." Thinking is very hard work; imagining — "making pictures" within the mind of things seen, heard, tasted, felt, smelt — is effortless: the pictures make themselves. Imagination and emotion are necessary human equipment, without them we should be barely two-dimensional; but they need to be controlled, and for each the way of control is different. Emotions are hard to control because of their violence, imagination because we are hardly aware of it. It is hard not to know — afterwards anyhow — what part emotion has had in what we thought were our judgments. It is easy to be totally unaware of what imagination has done to the picture of reality the intellect offers the will. And whereas we have to force ourselves into thinking, imagining just goes on — it never sleeps, and can be at its most vigorous when *we* sleep. Very early, immediately after the flood, Scripture warns us of its danger — "the imaginings of man's heart are evil from his youth" (Genesis 8:21).

The medieval traveler came back with stories of men with their heads under their arms. But that is surely a minor misshapenness (they had probably worked out a *modus vivendi*) compared with having our intellects under out imaginations. And whereas no traveler actually saw a head-under-shoulders man, we see about us intellect-under-imagination men, will-under-emotion men. I shave one every day.

I am not merely fooling; all that I have been saying goes into the values we live by, some good, some bad, but with only a catch-as-catch-can relation to reality, as liable to stunt and distort us as to make for our growth toward complete humanness.

Back to the will itself — the clutching, evading will. Odd as it may seem, self-interest is not the whole story: there is self-sacrifice too; men everywhere will die for a country or a cause. Illusory values can indeed draw the will, but real values can draw it too — when their value is seen *and felt*. Human beings are incalculable — you cannot rely on them even to be selfish. "A father's attitude to his children," I quote Chesterton from memory, "varies between something verging on idolatry, and something drifting towards infanticide."

Men may quite normally, unreflectingly, automatically almost, clutch or evade. Yet when some crisis forces them to face reality, they can draw extraordinary heroism from some depth in themselves that they never suspected. That is the point of one of the greatest of great short stories, Jack London's "The God of His Fathers."

And there is another facet of our incalculability, too complex to be more than mentioned here. It is a drawing to the irrational *as* irrational, to the negative *as* negative. Mere cussedness, and its next of kin, the cutting off of the nose to spite the face — these things are commonplace for many of us. Horace was wholly right when he said, "Temper is insanity while it lasts." Deeper still is the feeling Shelley utters, "We pine for what is not," the not-ness being the attraction. Perhaps.

II

Real values exist in relation to reality. But there is such a mass of reality that humanity cannot discover for itself with the eye of the body or even of the mind. We must be shown it or live in ignorance of it — to the inescapable confusion of our judgments on action and values.

For our present purpose, the most obvious example is the meaning of life. Life on earth is a road, not a dwelling: we are going, not staying. We are on the road; a while ago we were not; a longer while before no one was. In another while we shall no longer be on it; in an immeasurable while (the scientists tell us) no one will be. So what is it all abσut? Why are we here? Where (if anywhere) are we supposed to be going? How are we meant to get there? If we know the answers, we have all we need for value-judgments. If we do not, then we can only make guesses as to what suits people in general and ourselves in particular, very particular.

How *are* we to know? If there is a Mind at our origin; if this Mind reveals to us what the universe, and we in it, were made for, only then can we know. For the Christian, Christ has given the answer, has told us what we are, why we are, what our goal is and how we should reach it.

Without faith, the writer of Hebrews warns us, "it is impossible to please God": without faith, common sense warns us, it is impossible to live our lives intelligently. To be on a road and not know why we are on it or where it leads means to be lost — I don't mean eternally, but certainly for the duration of life on the road. To handle anything without knowing what it is *for* is folly — not less so if the thing we are handling thus blindly is ourself.

For most of us the question of how mankind got here is of no urgent concern. It belongs to the past; there is nothing we can do about it now. But what lies ahead, where the road leads that we are on — if there is any possibility of learning that, it would be strange to neglect it. From Christ we know that death is not the end, that there is a goal — a goal we may reach or fail to reach.

Believers have tended to think of the next life in terms of rewards or punishments, and indeed there is happiness in reaching the goal and misery in failure. But success or failure, happiness or misery have their roots in what we have made of ourselves. As I've said, in a sense perhaps deeper than Keats knew, our life here is a vale of Soul-making.

What is success? In the Greek word *teleios*, as adjective or noun or verb, the New Testament gives us the key. The difficulty is that Scripture's translators have used so many different English words for it (perhaps to avoid monotony) that we lose the cumulative effect of its frequency and the variety of its applications.

Take the account in John's 19th chapter of Christ's last moments on the cross. He had just given the disciple He loved to be a son to Mary. "After this Jesus, knowing that all was now *finished*, said (to *fulfill* the Scriptures), 'I thirst.' " Given vinegar, "he said 'It is *finished*'; and he bowed his head and gave up his spirit." *Telei* is the root of the verbs italicized: all of them are ways of saying "completed." It is the root also of the verb italicized in the following passage from Hebrews (5:8-9): "Although he was Son, he learnt obedience by the things he suffered; and being *made perfect*, he became the means of salvation to those who obey him." We have already felt the mystery in the idea of Christ being made perfect: clearly there was a new dimension needed for completeness of the humanity the redeemer must have.

Just as there was a completeness Christ must attain in order to redeem us, there is a completeness that we must attain to be redeemed: and it is still expressed in the same Greek word: "Do not be children in your thinking. Be babes in evil, but in your thinking be *mature*" (I Cor. 14:20). "Solid food is for the *mature*," says Hebrews (5:14); and at the beginning of chapter 6: "Let us leave the elementary doctrines of Christ and go on to *maturity*." "Him [Christ] we proclaim, warning every man and teaching every man in all wisdom, that we may present every man *mature* in Christ" (Col. 1:28). And Paul tells the Ephesians (4:12-13) of a larger purpose in the growing to completeness of each of us — "for the building up of the body of Christ, until we all attain to . . . *mature* manhood, to the measure of the stature of the fullness of Christ."

Whether it is Christ or the Church or ourselves, whether the word is translated as finished or fulfilled or perfect or mature, completeness is the basic meaning, nothing lacking that ought to be present. Colloquially we say that so-and-so is "all there." Praise indeed if it were true; it will not be true of any of us till we reach heaven.

In the Sermon on the Mount (Matthew 5:48) Christ has a double use of our key word which perhaps no one but He would have dared: "Be you also *perfect* as my heavenly Father is *perfect*." It is still the same idea of completeness — nothing missing that ought to be there. It was daring of Christ to bring God's perfection and man's into one statement. They are very different realities. Omniscience, omnipotence, infinite love, these belong to God's perfection, not to man's. Man's perfection lies in knowing and loving to the best of his capacity. Here on earth there is a provisional maturity as the heart seeks to know more and love more, not clinging to immaturity in either. Each new truth known enriches it. In the heart's direct union of knowledge with supreme truth, of loving with supreme goodness, we shall at last be complete men and women, not only the raw material out of which life is shaping us toward completion.

Love of God, love of man — heart functioning at its highest — Christ gives as the way to life. The other rules, including the Ten Commandments and many more growing out of the new reality He has revealed, He shows as ways of living by the first two or refusing them.

We can give our minds to the study of Christ and His message. In Paul's phrase we can have the mind of Christ and so be living mentally in the real world and in a condition to have true values. But our selves will still have to be coped with. Knowing the will of God, in full awareness of our own folly, we can sin — that is, we can grab the immediate pleasure and damn the consequences.

Disobeying the laws of reality always damages us — bodily and mentally. But sin — which is disobeying the moral laws built into the structure of our being by God in His making of us — damages our very selves as nothing else does. For it damages the mind we do our valuing with, leaving us with our values hopelessly distorted. We must not only repent our sins, and fight against the weakness of the will which yields to them; we must also bring our minds to bear more closely than ever on the values themselves.

III

The values we do try to live by are not entirely, or even mainly, of our own making; they are usually our individual combination of Christ's values with those of the society we were born into, with a garnish added of our personal tastes which may be very peculiar indeed. No two blades of grass, we are told, are exactly alike; we do not need to be told that no two hearts are.

It is a rare individual who questions values that his world takes for granted. Recently I was asked to lecture in South Australia on "The Challenge to Christian Integrity." I do not know what effect it had on the audience: it did nothing to cheer me.

The "challenge" of course is to ourselves. Can we be Christians in the world as it is without lots of small compromises, adaptings, which can add up in time to serious scalings down? Our examining of our conscience on these is not to be a searching for spectacular sins, for which most of us have not the physical or psychological equipment. Rather one should ask, What compromises with Christ's values have I made? How much have I cheapened myself thereby? AND FOR WHAT?

"Be not conformed to the world," St. Paul told the Romans but be transformed in newness of life" (Romans 12:2). And he reminded the Corinthians that the fashion of this world passes. Most people have an instinctive overall tendency to conform. Indeed life in any society large or small would be impossible if most people did not. And in all societies

there is a solid substratum of values, wholly real, wholly valuable. But in all there are "values" (and habits growing out of
them) which are more immediately exciting and more continually urging us, which add up to a pollution of the atmosphere we have to breathe. We are not forced to any outright
denial of Christ's values, but there are seepages, so to speak,
changes of emphasis. It can seem eccentric to go on regarding
conduct as unthinkable which our friends take for granted as
normal, especially when the friends seem such fine people (so
much more admirable, something whispers in us, than our
fellow Catholics).

An immense part of life as we and everybody else actually live it is made up of sex and money. Christ, we remember,
selected these two for special treatment. Both put our integrity
under continual pressure. Both are imperious — habit-form-
ing, self-forming.

I lectured a while ago in a Catholic college and was taken
out to dinner by the president. He drew my attention to two of
the waitresses and said they both had degrees from his college,
but could get no better jobs. He added with a sigh, "Four
years wasted." I felt he ought to know; it was his college. In
fact the incident was just one more reminder of the priority of
values in our world. Had he been reading a paper on educa-
tion, it would have been all about intellectual values. But
when he was just being himself, reality took over — his reality.

Love of money — money actually in the till, money in
the bank — is not so very common. Most people value it for
what they can do with it or what it can do for them. Only the

very rich are in danger of loving money for itself. But rich, or comfortably off, or poor — most of us are forced to pay a lot of attention to it. Christ saw the peril in it: "Where a man's treasure is, there is his heart." We should read Matthew 19:23 very carefully, weighing every word. We all know that he said "It is easier for a camel to go through the eye of a needle than for a rich man to enter the Kingdom of God" — it is in Matthew 19, Mark 10 and Luke 18. But we may have overlooked the dialogue that followed: the disciples questioned the astonishing words. He answered, "To man it is impossible; but to God all things are possible" — getting a camel through the eye of a needle, for instance, even (much harder, He says) getting a rich man into heaven.

And Judas, having heard all this, said to the chief priests, "How much will you give me if I deliver Him to you?"

Read again the parable of Dives and Lazarus (Luke 16:19 ff.). Dives means simply a rich man; it is not a personal name. Read every word — Dives feasting sumptuously while Lazarus waits at the gate, his sores licked by dogs; after death Dives in Hades tormented by thirst while Lazarus is in the place of honor at Abraham's banquet. Curiously, Christ is not forbidding or even attacking wealth, only warning against the heartlessness which can so easily go along with it. Money *can* be used rightly, can serve its owners and society's needs. But it can take possession so that we are serving it: Christ's warning is clear: "You cannot serve God and money." In our world Dives may be head of the parish council. Who else? The schools, hospitals, the poor of the parish — all need money; at least he understands money, knows about handling money.

Love of money seems to be what Christ is most concerned to warn us against — possibly with an eye to the Church's future. It is at least interesting that the first sin we are told of in the Church He founded was the money-sin of Ananias and Sapphira (Acts 5:1-11). And there is a bleak interest for us in learning that when Henry VIII confiscated the abbeys he got less than he had hoped since many of them were in the hands of money-lenders — because of the building mania of the abbots.

In our world as it is, money is valued as a status symbol. We actually hear the phrase, "So-and-so is worth a couple of million." *Worth!*

The advertisements can hardly fail to produce the feeling that you are inferior if your car is. Perhaps you do not feel it so: you are fortunate if your children don't. We cannot go on forever about this unfascinating subject. I leave it with two quotations. Thackeray defined a snob as "one who meanly admires mean things."

Mean things? Browning opens his poem "The Lost Leader" with two of them:

> *Just for a handful of silver he left us,*
> *Just for a riband to hang on his coat.*

Thomas Aquinas notes that avarice — love of money and money's purchasing power — has no natural limit. Rage, for instance, cannot forever preserve its first violence; the drunkard has to take time off from drinking to unsoak; even the lustful know what Shelley calls "love's sad satiety." What

Aquinas said about avarice Belloc summarizes — jestingly, but he is not only jesting:

> *I'm tired of love, I'm even tired of rhyme,*
> *But money gives me pleasure all the time.*

Sex has not the unrelaxing pressure of money, but at its height it can eclipse even money — can buy, for instance, what money cannot, as when Anne Boleyn became Queen of England. At its height, it has integrity at its mercy, men of honor no more to be trusted than rogues whom in any other area they would despise.

Oddly enough, standards of financial conduct have stood up better in our time than sexual. Even if people behave corruptly about money, no one defends financial corruption, still less boasts of his own thievery. In sex, on the other hand, there seem to be no standards left whose breach would be universally condemned as degradation.

I do not mean that our friends or neighbors have no sense left of sexual right or wrong. But when they are tempted to do something which once they would have thought sinful, they get no aid from public opinion; their world smiles at them for hesitating.

Why would they once have thought it sinful? Why, indeed, is it sinful? Quite apart from what their instincts or feelings may be, there are two evident facts.

There is first the simple fact that the sexual powers of men and women — so complex, so different, so delicately made for functioning together — would not have been there at all if human beings were not meant to procreate. This does not answer every question that may arise about the use of sex. But the total severance of the enjoyment of the sexual powers from the reason for our having them might well lead a thinking person to a mental as well as instinctive rejection of today's assumption that sex can do no wrong.

But second, even if there is no such clear rejection from within, there is the teaching of Christ, of special interest in our present study because He connects sex sin with the heart's corruption. In Mark's seventh chapter and Matthew's fifteenth, we have Him giving a list of sins that defile. It is a long list, and very early in it we find adultery, fornication (which is sexual union with no intention of permanence). They are defiling because, He emphasizes, they come "from within, out of the heart of a man."

Already, in the Sermon on the Mount, He had made clear that the commandment against adultery comdemned not only the bodily act — "anyone that looks at a woman lustfully has already committed adultery *in his heart*." Observe that there is not so much as a hint that He saw sex in itself as evil. He entered upon His public life with a miracle at a wedding feast. He affirmed that in marriage it is by God that the man and woman are joined together (Matthew 19); a verse or so earlier we find Him making His own the Genesis (2:23) statement that a husband and wife "become one flesh." He went further still: where Genesis leaves unclear whose words these were, Christ said that they were God's.

In fact it is with sex as with wealth — each has a right function. There is peril to the heart's purity in the misuse of each; there is an ultimate excellence in the refusal of each for something higher: with wealth, "If you would be perfect, sell all you have and give to the poor"; with sex, there are some who at God's call and for the sake of God's kingdom deny themselves the use of sex. Both these we find in that same 19th chapter of Matthew.

Christ's mind is clear. But sex goes on clamoring, and our world has canonized its clamors. For Christendom, this vanishing of sex standards from what we may call public opinion really is a new situation.

There is something eerie about the total calmness with which the American public has accepted the news that in the first year of legalized abortion a million babies were slain in the womb by men paid by their mothers to slay them. An authority in one area was beaming because there were a quarter million abortions "and not one life lost." When Christians or Jews object to the killing of a million infants, they are told that they must not interfere with the freedom of others: after all, the infants don't know — and anyhow the objectors are not compelled to practice abortion. Not yet! But there is already a movement to put a limit — a low limit — on the number of children any couple may have. The notion of sex as sacred — a cooperation with God in the production of beings made in His image, destined for everlasting life — when did anyone last hear that?

I am not discussing the absence of legislation on sex practices so recently thought abominable. It is the absence of public opinion on the matter that is really scaring. A clergyman on England's BBC said that he uses pornographic material to counsel the lonely as it comforts them, enabling them to perform obscene acts in safety. A bishop, not of our Church, has just ordained to the priesthood a lady who went on the air to tell how spiritually helpful she found her lesbianism. We are moving back in the direction of the ritual copulation of the pre-Christian pagans with their male and female Temple prostitutes. The next "world religion" will probably be built around it.

All this raises the problem of the Christian family in a society with no sex standards left. It is grim to have one's children mixing freely with their sexually promiscuous little friends, attending parties at which sex games are played. Christians who believe Christ's teaching that sex when misused defiles the user are being forced morally into a ghetto. They might manage to live that way themselves, but they will find it hard to force it on their children — when the children are longing to do what everyone else does and their parents cannot very lucidly or convincingly tell them why they shouldn't.

This is the world that Paul warns us not to be conformed to — not the world so much as what Paul calls "the fashion of this world" — in fact its worldliness, its abiding tendency to handle life without reference to God, the clutching, evading will of mankind set upon shaping reality to its own wishes.

Paul urges us not to be conformed to the world. Thomas More prayed: "Give me grace, dear Lord, to set the world at naught." The world does not easily forgive those who set it at naught. It beheaded both Paul and More.

Postscript to Chapter Three

Till the day before yesterday — say up to ten years ago — the mark of our world was self-assurance. The human race, it felt, had reached maturity. There were still problems, of course. But science was at work; the sum of human knowledge doubled every ten years, or was it five? "Mankind has come of age," said that notable man Pastor Bonhoeffer, just before Hitler hanged him.

The self-assurance has vanished — almost overnight. Only the dullest can fail to see that the world seems to be passing out of even that strictly provisional control mankind thought it had. Crises multiply, and the solution to all of them seems to be bloodshed. This is already the bloodiest century in history. There were two world wars, the Spanish Civil War, millions of Russians allowed by Stalin to starve in the thirties, millions of Jews cremated by Hitler, a couple of hundred thousand Japanese slain by us in a couple of flashes, deaths beyond counting in Indonesia, in Uganda, in Vietnam, torture returning everywhere with new techniques. And none of these millions of killings brought security to the killers.

Maturity? It would be hard to question Vatican II's sober judgment that mankind has reached a crisis point on its way to maturity. When we read of Christ's compassion on the multitude, "harassed and helpless like sheep without a shepherd," which of us would feel certain that the description does not fit his own country, whichever it is?

There are signs of panic everywhere, rulers everywhere finding it harder to cope, reduced to emergency measures with more than a hint of desperation in them. In our own world, money, the life-blood of the system, functions dizzily: to say that a man has a sterling character used to mean that he was reliable; who relies now on England's pound? And who knows what the dollar will be worth tomorrow?

With whatever wrappings of words in speeches or laws, what Wordsworth called the "good old rule, the simple plan" still is

> *That they should take who have the power,*
> *And they should keep who can.*

But the lawless can no longer walk sure-footed any more than the lawgivers can, or the exploiters any more than the exploited. Chaos is not here; but uncertainty, its forerunner, is already settling in. I told earlier of a diamond merchant who invested all his profits in stamps. But how long can you trust stamps?

Trust indeed is the test word of society's health. People no longer trust the governments they elect; labor mistrusts management, neither trusting its own leaders. Who is on whose side when the ground is rocking? A society lives by agreement on values, but what agreed values are there in our own society? What fundamental principles? And without such principles, what basis is there for trust? Who would want to conform, to be in step with a society marching so uncertainly, to be in tune with a society too unsure to sing?

In the so sure world of yesterday, there were even convinced Christians, accepting for their personal lives Christ's values and priorities, to whom it did not occur that these same values and priorities were essential in social, political, economic life; to whom it was a new idea, for instance, when Pope Paul said that Christ's command to feed the hungry was as binding on nations as on individuals.

The loss of confidence in man's power to run his world leaves an opening for Christ which barely existed before, an opening above all to the truth that the world is not man's but God's. In the high summer of human progress, Christ's two-fold rule — love of God and love of neighbor — was dismissed as baby talk, not for modern man. But modern man is not feeling so well, and Christ was no baby. What the world needs with new urgency are Christians who realize the practicality here and now of Christ's message and *who can communicate it*. Though the human mind was mistaken in thinking that it could solve all the problems of the world, it was a magnificent instrument, and there have been rich developments in its thinking through the last century and a half. If only Christian thinkers could give their minds to bringing these developments into union with the mind of Christ.

Will they do so?

God knows.

In that answer there is no irreverence but all hope.

The
Heart
of Mary

CHAPTER FOUR

The Heart of Mary

I hesitated before beginning this book with an individual heart, the one I knew best. I have no hesitation at all about ending it with the heart of Jesus' Mother: for our topic is the instructed heart, and no heart ever had the instructors hers had. For an additional reason, it was her habit to keep things *in her heart* that puzzled her and to ponder on them. Too many of those who love her seem to have switched off their intellects, leaving emotion to have a carnival. Newman warns us that we do not honor her by saying things in her praise which can only be explained by being explained away. She was the Virgin Mother of God: nothing is left in that for rhetoric's gilding but everything for the mind's exploring. The surest way is to see what things she kept in her heart and to ponder on them ourselves.

My main concern here will be with things she pondered. The Church of her Son tells us that she had sanctifying grace in her soul from the moment of her conception in the womb of her mother. It tells us too that at her death she was taken into heaven, body and soul united. These two doctrines I shall assume but not discuss: if she learnt of them in this life, then there must have been considerable pondering, with not much light from existent Scripture; but we hear no word of this, and in what we do hear there is plenty for pondering, for us as for her.

I

Read Luke 1:26-58 and the first two chapters of Matthew. Luke tells of God sending an angel to "a virgin betrothed to a man whose name was Joseph, of the House of David." Betrothal was not, as with us, an engagement to marry. It meant that the man and the girl — she usually about twelve or thirteen — had taken each other for husband and wife; in Matthew's Gospel Joseph and Mary are called so. But by Jewish custom they did not begin their life together at once: each returned home for a year; then the husband came with his relatives and friends, musicians perhaps and torches, to the wife's house to bring her to his own; after that came the feasting; and that was that. Normally the two did not have bodily union in the intervening year — it would be unusual in Galilee, less so in Judea. But if they did, it was not a sin, and the child born of the union was legitimate.

At some point during that year the angel came to Mary in Nazareth. His opening words were "Hail, full of grace, the Lord is with you." Here we have her first puzzlement. "She cast about in her mind what sort of greeting this might be." "Hail" was no problem, though Old Testament angels had no habit of calling on women. But there is no record of anyone having been greeted as "full of grace." So what did it mean? Catholics assume that "grace" here means sanctifying grace, the indwelling of God in the soul. But Mary would not have found that idea in the Old Testament. Her Son would tell of it. "Full of grace." It sounded like a term of praise, and the angel made clear that it was.

He went on:

> *You have found favor with God. And you shall conceive in your womb and bear a son, and you shall call his name Jesus.*
> *He will be great and will be called the Son of the Most High.*
> *And the Lord God will give him the throne of his father David.*
> *And he will reign over the house of Jacob forever;*
> *And of his kingdom there will be no end.*

It was a promise of measureless glory, but Mary saw a problem: "How can this be? I know not man." "Know" was a scriptural idiom for sexual union: "Adam knew Eve his wife, and she conceived and brought forth Cain. . . ." But, we ask, "What about Joseph, her legal husband? Could she not go on to have the promised child by him?" Her remark makes sense only on one condition — that when Gabriel said, "You shall conceive," he meant "immediately," here and now. The Church seems always to have assumed that that was his meaning, celebrating the announcement made by Gabriel on March 25th and Christ's birth exactly nine months later.

The angel answered:

> The Holy Spirit will come upon you,
> and the power of the Most High will overshadow you;
> therefore the child to be born of you will be called
> Holy,
> the Son of God.

As a reminder that nothing is impossible to God, Gabriel told of the miracle by which Mary's aged relative Elizabeth had conceived a son. And Mary said, "I am the handmaid of the Lord; be it done to me according to your word." Those were the words of consecration by which she brought God the Son into our race.

This happens to be the longest conversation recorded of Mary — in it she speaks twice, hardly twenty words. It may have been longer in its happening, of course. What did she make of it? She had been puzzled by the opening words, but they were a trifle compared with what was to come. She was to conceive a son not in the way of marriage but by a miracle of God's power, virginally; there was nothing to prepare her for that in the Old Testament, with its absence of virgins — nor, if she had known them, in the pagan myths, which had improbable births in plenty but not a virgin birth in the lot, only ingenious tricks by which lustful gods had their way with reluctant women.

She could hardly have failed to know that her child was to be the Messiah: Jesus means "God saves"; but what did "Son of the Most High" and "Son of God" mean? The doctrine of the Trinity is not revealed in the Old Testament. Jews holding special offices had been called Sons of God, so had Jews of special piety. But a messenger from God and a virginal conception must have meant more than that. She had mysterious words to keep in her heart and ponder on.

And one question she simply must have asked — "Why me?"

Two things — one that she did immediately and one that she didn't — give us matter for pondering: she didn't tell Joseph, but she did start "in haste" on the ninety-mile journey into the hills of Judea to visit her aged kinswoman Elizabeth, so incredibly pregnant — with John the Baptist, who was to be the forerunner of Mary's own child.

Clearly Mary's design in coming had been to help, and she stayed three months, which would have brought her up to the birth of Elizabeth's baby. But Elizabeth gave her more things for pondering, three especially. First, in greeting she had said, "Blessed are you among women." Mary would have known the phrase. The Old Testament has it twice for women who had saved God's people — Jael, wife of Heber, by hammering a tent peg into the skull of the enemy leader Sisera (Judges 4:17-5:24); and Judith (13:22, 15:10), a widow, by cutting the head off the enemy leader Holofernes. Did Mary know about the son (Genesis 3:15) who was to crush a head of greater malignity than the heads of Sisera and Holofernes combined? Second, Elizabeth had addressed Mary as "the mother of my Lord." Gabriel had said to Zachary (Zechariah) that Elizabeth's son would "convert many of the children of Israel to the *Lord* their *God.*" When Elizabeth said "Lord" here, did she mean "God"?

Third was the "leaping" of the child in Elizabeth's womb at the sound of Mary's voice. It was the first reaction to Jesus by His forerunner.

In three months the two women had incredible things to tell each other. But we have not a word of their conversation. The Magnificat, spoken by Mary, was not spoken to Elizabeth. How much does it tell of Mary's heart? It contains passages from the Old Testament, mainly from the prayer prayed by Hannah, mother of the prophet Samuel, after his birth (Samuel 2:1-10). Read it and the Magnificat (Luke 1:46-55) in turn. There are similarities, but the differences are notable — one of Hannah's phrases, "My mouth derides my enemies," Mary does not, could not, make her own.

Nor could Hannah conceivably have said, "All generations shall call me blessed." Said by a carpenter's wife from a small town in Galilee, it would sound ridiculous — if it had not happened. On anyone's lips it would have sounded boastful. But Mary's humility was utterly real. Here, as in the acceptance of Gabriel's message, the English version has her call herself "handmaid" of the Lord. The Greek has *doule* — slave.

II

Back to Nazareth. Read the first two chapters of Matthew's Gospel. The news of her pregnancy had reached Joseph. Why had she not told him? It may have been her feeling that a mystery of such magnitude should be told only by God. More simply they may not have met in the interval. We do not know where he was living; his later settlement in Nazareth was an afterthought. The secret, which might have been possible to tell face to face, she might have found impossible to tell in writing. Ponder his anguish till "in a dream" an angel told him, "Fear not to take Mary your wife, for that which is conceived in her is of the Holy Spirit; she will have a son, and you shall call his name Jesus, for he will save his people from their sins."

So the wedding took place. Joseph brought her, visibly pregnant, to his home. There must have been plenty of jesting about her condition. This husband and wife were not easy talkers, either of them: what anyhow could they say? Bodily union would not have been sinful: it was perhaps assumed that Joseph had visited her during her three months in Judea: whatever talk there was must have died down quickly, for Jesus was never taunted with it. But it must have been a grim time for the twelve-year-old girl. Had it been breathed that Joseph was not the father she might well have been stoned.

But only Joseph knew, and he accepted the child as his own, circumcising Him and naming Him, thus making himself legally the father of Jesus as he was legally the husband of Mary, giving Jesus legally a descent from David, even had He not been physically so through His mother. We are not told that Mary was a descendant of David. It would be hard to believe she was not, in the light of other utterances about her Son — Peter's "fruit of David's loins," Paul's "of the seed of David according to the flesh."

It could not have been easy for any of the three. Some aged relative would be sure to remark that the child was the very image of Joseph at the same age — someone always sees nonexistent likenesses. One way or another situations must continually have arisen, things been constantly said, with silence the only refuge. And silence gets noticed.

I rush over the birth in Bethlehem, told by Matthew in his second chapter and depicted in thousands of paintings with not much regard to first-century clothing or ways of acting — the wise men from the east turned into kings, but probably professor types. Our subject being what it all meant to Mary, we pause at three points — the reports of the shepherds, which "Mary kept . . . pondering them in her heart"; the words of the learned Simeon, at which the child's "father and mother marvelled"; and the "gifts of gold and frankincense and myrrh."

The shepherds told of the angel who had said, "To you is born this day in the city of David a Savior who is Christ the Lord" — nothing new to Mary or Joseph in that. The shepherds went on to tell of a multitude of angels and their chant, "Glory to God in the highest."

Religiously and socially hill-shepherds were at the very bottom, their word not accepted in a court of law. The professors from the East ranked higher, but they were not even Jews. Like Anna, Simeon was a frequenter of the Temple, notably holy. Yet not of the establishment, not of the priesthood, not of the Sanhedrin. We are not told if Mary wondered why God had not informed the High Priest of the coming of His Son into our world; surely she must have.

Simeon's opening words, spoken with the child Jesus in his arms, were a cry of gratitude to God for letting him end his life in peace, having seen the Savior. They could have loved him for that. But the phrase that followed — "[this is] a light for revelation to the Gentiles and the glory of your people Israel" — with the mention of the Gentiles first, gave them at least a mild shock: thirty years later their Son's insistence on this same priority would make their townsfolk try to kill Him.

The next words introduce a wholly new note — that it will not be all glory: "This child is destined to bring about the rise and fall of many in Israel, a sign to be spoken against." So the Gospel would not be good news to all, even of Israel. Then a prophecy about Mary herself — "your own soul a sword shall pierce, that thoughts out of many hearts may be revealed." It sounds like a promise of agony for her: but what had the piercing of her heart to do with the revealing of thoughts out of many hearts?

More than half a century later, the Epistle to the Hebrews will link a sword with the laying open of thoughts of the heart: "The word of God (*ho logos tou theou*) is living and active, sharper than any two-edged sword, piercing to the division of the soul and spirit . . . and discerning the thoughts and intentions of the heart. And before him no creature is hidden, but all are open and laid bare to the eyes of him with whom we have to do" (Hebrews 4:12-13). Mary and Joseph had not read that still-to-be-written Epistle, nor had Simeon; but surely the writer of Hebrews had heard the words of Simeon, whether from Luke's Gospel or from Mary herself. We, who *have* read Hebrews, wonder whether Simeon's words promise suffering or revelation — or both? For then as now knowledge can make a bloody entry.

One of the gifts the learned men from the east brought must have left them in some doubt of its significance. All their gifts were strange. Gold was normal for kings; incense could be offered only to gods, but myrrh! It was a fragrant resin, always associated with death — used in embalming by the Egyptians, sprinkled on dead bodies by the Jews — strange as a gift to a newborn child.

What did either the angels or Simeon or the learned men add to what had already been shown them? What in fact *had* been shown them? My emphasis here is on the word "shown" — not what had been said to them, but what it had meant to them.

At a minimum, they knew that by the power of God Mary had conceived virginally and given birth to a son whom the angel had called "the Son of the Most High"; and with the same certainty but greater comprehension they knew that her son was to be the Messiah — greater comprehension, because a ruler of Israel who should save his people from their sins was not so difficult to imagine. But for the God of Israel to have a son of His own — what meaning could they make of that? The gods of the Gentiles were highly sexed and had sons and daughters a-plenty. But there was no sex in Israel's God. What indeed does it mean to us that a *spirit* should have a son?

In the opening of John's Gospel we can read that God utters a Word, a Word which is God. Of a phrasing so mysterious men's minds have made just about every thinkable variation. But the Church Christ founded, and with it almost all the churches separated from it through the centuries, have held to an interpretation in which no word of John's phrasing is sacrificed, every word seen as essential.

If the one God utters a word it cannot be of the human sort, a word made of air expelled from the lungs and shaped by the tongue and teeth and lips; it can only be a "word" in the divine mind, a mental word, a word whose uttering consists in being thought, a concept. John tells us that this Word, conceived in God's mind, is itself God. What thought *could* be God? Only God's thought of Himself.

So Christians have seen it. God, knowing Himself with infinite knowing power, conceives the totally perfect idea of Himself, lacking no excellence that God Himself has — eternal as He is eternal, Someone as He is someone, God as He is God. We may think of this second Someone as the Son generated, or as the Word uttered, or as the Idea conceived, by the First — but generated or conceived or uttered eternally, since God's existence is not in time. In verse 14 John says that the "Word became flesh and dwelt among us." And we saw His glory as of the only Son of God, the fullness of grace and truth — the Word, possessing the divine nature eternally, made a human nature His own, conceived by Mary as we all are conceived — an infant in the womb, born of her, growing to adulthood. At the opening of his first epistle John would one day write of "That which was from the beginning, which we have seen with our eyes . . . and touched with our hands . . . the eternal life which was with the Father and was made manifest. . . ."

John, remember, was "the disciple Jesus loved"; he lay next to Jesus at the last supper, was given by Jesus as son to Mary, and took her to his home afterwards. How much did she add to what John had already learnt from her Son? More to our present point is, how much of it had she already known at Bethlehem? How much of the Holy Spirit, who proceeded from Father and Son? And how had she come to know it? By using her mind on what had been said to her? Or by further revelation from God?

Here everyone will answer as seems most probable to the kind of person he is. That is what I proceed to do. For me, only if God revealed it would it be thinkable that He had taken a girl and used her simply as a convenience to get His Son conceived into our humanity, without telling her the why and the wherefore, and who and what the baby was. She had to do something no one had ever done — bring up a child who was God. It would help her to know what she was doing; it would help Joseph too, who had a husband's rights. How much light from above would that take? Enough, at least, to know what the message contained. Father, Son and Holy Spirit — the three were in the message, but it would be hard to find the Trinity in their Scriptures. Mary and Joseph, Jesus too, in His human mind, could know it only if revealed to them.

III

But how would it all work out? Perhaps, that she might be left to find out for herself, as the rest of us have to find out how God's indwelling in ourselves by baptism is going to work out.

Soon enough she knew of the two natures in her child. Divinity was in her womb — but at His first stirring within her, she knew she had conceived a real baby. In that you have the whole problem. She and Joseph had to bring to maturity One who was true God and real baby — as God omnipotent, as baby wholly dependent. If she had been too much in awe of His divinity to wash Him, to feed Him, He would have gone unwashed, unfed.

But how continue to realize the divinity of a being who needed washing and needed feeding — who may have needed comforting when He cried. The problem is not so remote from ourselves: we know that in the Eucharist Christ is really present, body and blood and soul and divinity: if we were too stricken with awe to open our mouths, our souls would go unnourished; but how realize a divinity we can receive in our mouths?

For us, the problem is solved in the living of it: it sounds impossible as said; it is wonderfully possible as happening. For them too? The child, being a real child, had to be taught. Handling omnipotence is one thing; teaching omniscience is another. What must it have felt like to be teaching a divine Person His prayers? With a couple of thousand years to ponder, we can see how in our own experience knowledge comes to us not from our person but from our nature — reality flowing through the senses to the brain where the mind takes hold of it and so at last I, the person I am, know it. Are we to assume that, in this one Being, there was a counterflow, knowledge from the divine personality that was His bringing light to the humanity that was His? Only the God-man can tell us that.

IV

When, with Bethlehem and Jerusalem and Egypt behind them, the three settle in Nazareth, we lose sight of them for thirty years, save for a single episode in Jerusalem when the boy was twelve.

There is a way of calling this disappearance into Nazareth "the hidden life." It would hardly have occurred to them to use the phrase. A carpenter's shop in a village would not have been a retreat, a place of withdrawal from the world. Most of it was open to the street, with strangers looking in and acquaintances coming in whenever they felt like it. Save late at night and early in the morning, there would have been no privacy at all.

And the three had so much more to talk about, to clarify their own relation to, than any three had ever had. There is no record of their conversation, not so much as a word; we cannot help speculating about it, which is all to the good provided that we don't forget that we are speculating. Two saints and a child who was God might easily have found things to say to each other special to themselves, outside our guessing range.

There was the virginity of Joseph and Mary, for example, accepted by both in the light of what each had learnt from God. It is not inconceivable that their love for each other might have reached a splendor which would have made bodily union an anticlimax.

What to me is inconceivable is that they should not have talked freely among themselves — Mary and Joseph from the beginning, Jesus as He grew older — about what God had wrought in them. The things Mary had kept in her heart and pondered could now be freely expressed.

Yet the single incident when the boy was twelve is a reminder to us that there was a depth not only beyond our reach but past Mary's too. For the last time we hear of something she kept in her heart.

Jesus had made the ninety-mile journey to the Temple with Mary and Joseph for Passover. On the return journey they discovered that He was not, had not been, of the party. They retraced their steps, looking for Him; found Him at last in the sort of group which gathered daily round learned men in the Temple. The boy was not teaching them, of course: He was following the normal pattern of such groups — answering the rabbi's questions, putting questions of His own — but with such brilliance that all were "astonished." (The Greek word literally means "taken out of themselves.") His parents were more astonished still — the Greek here is equivalent to "electrified."

His mother said, "Why have you done this to us? Your father and I have been looking for you sorrowing." His answer was, "Why did you search for me? Didn't you know that I must be in my Father's" — His Father's what? "In my Father's house," the Temple, would be an obvious guess. "In my Father's service," or "concerns," attending to some work

His Father wanted Him to do, is yet another suggestion.*

One thing is certain: we do not now know exactly what He meant. Another thing is probable: Mary and Joseph did not know then — "they did not understand the saying that he said to them."

Look close at their problem. Mary had spoken of Joseph and herself as "your father and I": the boy's answer bypassed Joseph, went straight to His eternal Father. Was this the first time? Had He always called Joseph His father in Nazareth? The Jews knew God as their Father but it was not their habit to speak of God as "my Father." If it was the first time it must indeed have been electrifying to Mary to hear *her* son speaking of God as "my Father."

Their son's answer really bypassed her question too, for it gave an answer she could not interpret. If He meant the Temple, there was no mystery in the phrase, but it shed no light on why He had stayed on for three days without telling them. If He really meant "in my Father's service," they were facing something they did not know and that He did not intend to tell them. "And he went down with them and came to Nazareth and was obedient to them; and his mother kept all these things in her heart."

It may be that what had first astounded her and Joseph in the Temple was Jesus' showing His brilliance. Clearly He

———

*Luke (2:49) has *en tois tou Patros mou*, a usage we lack in English; literally it reads "in the (things?) of my Father." Irenaeus, in the second century, uses exactly the same five Greek words in quoting John 14:2, where John has "in the house of my Father."

had given no past evidence of uniqueness in Nazareth, nor did He do so in the next eighteen years. Why didn't she ask the boy about the things that puzzled her? But in the Temple she had asked Him and had been given no light. It looked as if He had a work to do which would not be hers, in the service of a Father who was not Joseph. What indeed *was* her function — to conceive Him, bear Him into the world, feed Him, clothe Him, rear Him to maturity, then what? It was a development of the question she must have had in her heart at the Annunciation — "Why me?"

She had close on twenty years to ponder it. Life went on. The boy "increased in wisdom and in stature and in favor with God and man." He was a carpenter's son; He became a carpenter Himself (Mark 6:3). Joseph died. A new lot of cousins enter the picture. Hebrew and Aramaic having no word for "cousin," they were called brothers and sisters — terms used for any close relations (just like the French word "parents"). We know the names of four of the cousins — James, Joseph, Simon, Judas (Matthew 13:55) — and we know the name of the mother of the first two, "Mary, the mother of James and Joseph." She was at Calvary (Matthew 27:55) with the mother of Jesus and saw where Christ was laid in the tomb (Mark 15:47).

There seems to have been nothing in all these years to draw any special attention to Jesus either in the town or at home. When around the age of thirty, He began to work miracles — in other towns, mostly — the people of Nazareth found it hard to believe (Matthew 13:54). "Isn't this the carpenter's son? Isn't his mother called Mary? And these brothers

and sisters of his?" Where could He have acquired the learning He had shown in the Synagogue? They just could not accept Him. On His final visit they tried to kill Him (Luke
4:28-30).

Jesus' comment is, "A prophet is not without honor ex-
cept in his own country and in his own house." In his own
house? The cousins do not show up well at this stage (the first
two were to become Apostles, James and Simon). We shall
meet them shortly. So far He had not made much more impression on them than on the rest of Nazareth.

It seems to have been a long, incredibly long, private life
for one who had a world to redeem. It looks as if, but for
Mary, it might have been even longer. Read what happened at
a marriage feast in Cana, four miles from Nazareth (John 2).
A while before Jesus had been baptized in the Jordan, one of
thousands. Four or five men had felt drawn to follow Him. He
took them to the party in Cana where His mother was. The
rest can be told quickly. We shall not quickly exhaust its
meaning. Mary told her Son that there was no wine left. His
answer John gives in the Greek of his Gospel:

> *TI EMO KAI SOI ESTIN, GUNE*
> *What to me and to you is it, Woman*

Back in the teens and twenties of this century when
Maisie Ward and I were new at teaching religion under the
open sky, this sentence was a no-popery showpiece, translated
as "Woman, what have I to do with thee?", a repudiation by
the Savior of His Mother! I remember how patiently we

would explain to the questioner that two thousand years ago language had not developed to the point where "Woman" was a term of contempt. (A friend of mine found it not contemptuous enough — if he disliked a lady he would refer to her as "that female woman.") This sort of elementary explanation is not often called for now; when it is, we remind the questioner that Christ addressed His Mother with the same word on Calvary, when He was giving the disciple He loved to be her son.

But even scholars seem to lose their balance a little on "what have I to do with thee." They point out that, in the dozen or so other places it is used in the two Testaments, that is a reasonable translation. A more balanced reader would notice: (a) that in practically all the other instances there was real hostility (as when demons said it to Jesus), and in all of them a strong division of opinion, whereas "What have I to do with thee" is meaningless from a son to a mother; (b) that while verbally His answer sounded like NO, especially when Jesus went on to say, "My hour is not yet come," her Son did in fact work the miracle she was asking for and she knew He would. "Son, they have no wine" is only the second thing we are told of her saying to her Son, and we never hear of another; it is worth lingering on it. Why did she assume that Jesus could work the miracle? I know what my guess is; your guess is as good.

After His apparent refusal she said to the waiters, "Do whatever he tells you" — as this is the last thing we ever hear her say to anyone at all, it is worth a moment: surely if she had had a whole lifetime to choose her last words, she could hardly have chosen better. It was the rule of her own heart, her message for all hearts. Why, we may wonder, did she brush aside His statement that His hour had not yet come? It can only mean that the embarrassment of the bride on the great day of her life seemed to Mary sufficient reason for her Son's hour (whatever that meant) to advance its coming. She really cared for that girl and her parents.

What did "His hour" mean? The hour for His showing Himself to the world. The one certain way to do that was to work a public miracle. A known miracle-worker becomes public property. Even the small privacy of Nazareth would be gone. At Bethlehem she had ushered Him into life; at Cana she ushered Him into public life. She must have known that the world would move in on Him. Did she know how totally? There is no sure indication that she and her Son met again till He was crucified, just over two years later, on Calvary. Her instinct had been right so long ago in the Temple: He *had* a work to do in which there would as yet be no direct part for her.

There were the Apostles, seven more to join Cana's five. There were "the women who had been healed of evil spirits and infirmities — Mary called Magdalene . . . and Joanna the wife of Chuza, Herod's steward, Susanna and many others, who provided for them [Christ and the Twelve] out of their means" (Luke 8:3). The Mary who was mother of James and Simon sometimes went with them. But Jesus' mother stayed at home, with the rest of the cousins: after all, prophets were not in the habit of taking their mothers with them; and she was not yet part of His message — she became so on Calvary.

Those cousins must have been a trial. They did not

believe in Him, John tells us (7:5). They had come to know that He had some mysterious powers, of healing, for instance. But they thought Him unbalanced (Mark 3:21), working miracles in a backwater like Galilee instead of in Judea. He needed someone, not only to take care of Him, but to handle His career. He needed good public relations men. Even one of the cousins who became an Apostle, Jude, had something of this feeling almost to the end — at the Last Supper he asked "How is it that you show yourself to us *and not to the world?*" Their urgency brought upon Mary what must have seemed to everybody a slap in the face from her Son.

He was in a house in Capernaum, the crowds thronging. The message was brought to Him that His mother and His brethren were outside asking to see Him. Do you really think that *she* sent that message in? Surely it came from the public relations group! Anyhow the answer was: "Who is my mother and who are my brethren? . . . Whoever does the will of my Father in heaven is my brother and sister and mother" (Matthew 12:46-50).

To the cousins it must have seemed like the end — He had abandoned Nazareth; it seemed that He was disowning them, even disowning His mother. What did it mean to her? To all who have learnt from her Son, what He said is the obvious truth. Physical relationship is not the primary reality about anyone; it may be no more than a biographical fact; relationship in grace, which comes from doing God's will, affects everything in us — what we do, the direction of our life, what we are. Any relation in grace is closer than any in blood. We are all more closely related to one another as members of

Christ's Body than to our own blood kin — our mothers, for example: though my own mother, yours too, I hope, was a member of His Body; I could not but marvel at the intensity of her love for Him.

This truth is so elementary that Mary must have known it. She would not have had to wait till St. Augustine put it on paper — "More blessed is she in receiving Him by faith than in conceiving Him in her womb." Elementary indeed, but not often realized. And Jesus had a particular reason for reminding the Jews of it — given their conviction that their Jewish blood left the Gentiles forever inferior. For Jews and Gentiles the test is doing the will of God: in Christ, Paul tells the Galatians (3:28), there is no distinction of Jew or Greek, slave or free, male or female — all are one person (*eis*) in Christ Jesus. As he puts it to the Colossians (3:11), "Christ is all in all."

It was the most difficult lesson for His hearers to learn, even after Pentecost the Apostles still had not fully learnt it. In this matter of blood relationship, a woman in the crowd gave Jesus one further opportunity, crying "Blessed is the womb that bore you and the breasts that suckled you" (Luke 11:27). She was not thinking of His mother — who was probably not even there; it looks as if the episode took place in Judea. The woman was using a normal formula in praise of *Him*. But Jesus went beyond it, "Blessed rather are those who hear the word of God and keep it." It was a truth not grasped by the tenth century and Renaissance popes with their frenzy for the enrichment of their relatives. I wonder if Barnabas may have forgotten it when he had that scene with Paul — a "paroxism," Acts 15:39 calls it — because he thought Paul was being unfair to Mark (who happened to be Barnabas's nephew).

Mary understood the reason for the two-year separation. Her Son had a work to do — redeeming and revealing. In neither was she needed. And she had uttered at Cana her own rule of life — "Do whatever he tells you." But seeing why does not prevent suffering. A mother is not merely a contrivance to get a child born. The relation is unique and does not end for mother or child at the child's birth. It is lifelong, eternal-lifelong. One of love's inseparables, human love or divine, is the desire to be with, to converse with, share with, rejoice with, suffer with. The desire abides, it belongs to love. But the actual being-with may be prevented — by death, for instance — and pain is inescapable, pain of loss, pain of absence.

Did she and her Son not meet between Cana and Calvary? If they did not, why did He choose it so? I do not pretend to know. I can theorize, we can all theorize, but only if He tells can we know. What about the pain the long absence caused her? Was there any point in that? And did it mean nothing to Him?

We cannot understand His life or hers or our own without seeing clearer about their suffering. His, for instance. Was it really necessary? Hebrews (5:8) answers with almost mathematical precision, "Though He was Son, He learnt obedience by the things He suffered. And being made perfect, He became the means of salvation to those who obey Him, being designated by God a high priest after the order of Melchizedek." There was no statable, utterable, truth about obedience that He needed to learn; but there is a deeper understanding

— a fourth dimension — to be gained by suffering unto death, and that way lies perfection. Without the loving acceptance by the will of suffering for God's sake, Christ could not have reached His own perfection, therefore could not have been our Redeemer. So says Hebrews.

V

This was the truth Paul applied to himself so startlingly in Colossians (1:24): "I rejoice in my sufferings for your sake, and in my flesh I complete what is lacking in Christ's afflictions for the sake of his body, the Church." At a glance we have two shocks here — something lacking to Christ's sufferings for the Church, Paul offering his own suffering to make up the lack. In what Christ Himself did, nothing was lacking. But we are not to be spectators at our own redemption, cheering Him on in His agony, ourselves not agonizing. There is a part we *must* play, offering our sufferings in union with His.

This is where we find Our Lady. After all, neither we nor Paul can offer the whole of our sufferings for the salvation of others: some at least of ours, to say nothing of Paul's, must be applied by Christ to the cleansing of the damage our own sins have done to us. She at least had no sins to call for any subtraction from the sufferings she offers to Christ for His Church. But what had she to offer? Her suffering in her Son's suffering, of course. But she had, as we all have, suffering on her own account — in Joseph's death, for example, and in Elizabeth's. There was the loss of His outward presence; the happiness of that she had known as no one else has ever known it — the daily sharing, the signs of affection, the whole atmosphere. It would take an abler writer than I am to convey what this would mean, especially to a mother who knew of the enemies surrounding her Son, and of the grievous death which was moving relentlessly in on Him. But is there any need to convey the pain of the separation which only ended when she saw her Son nailed to the cross?

In the light of all this we see the answer to the question forced on us by His words to her on Calvary, "Woman, behold your son," and His words to John, the disciple He loved, "Behold your mother." These two were the last human beings He spoke to as He was dying. If it was merely a provision for His mother, left childless by His own death, it is very touching, of course. But why did He choose that moment? He had known for long enough that He would die. He knew that He would have forty days of risen life on earth.

Very early the Church saw that He did not interrupt the sacrifice of the world's redemption merely to make a sensible arrangement for His mother's earthly well-being. (John did "take her to his own home.") The Church came to see from the timing that it had to be part of the action of our redemption. John was the first member of the human race offered by Christ to her motherhood. "After this," says John, "Jesus, knowing that all was now completed, said, to fulfill the Scriptures, 'I thirst.' They put a sponge full of vinegar to his mouth. Whereupon Jesus said, 'It is finished,' bowed his head and gave up his spirit."

So, as Hebrews tells us, by His sufferings He was made

114   *The Instructed Heart*

perfect. So by her sufferings she was made perfect — with her own part to play in the application of Calvary to every sinner, as Paul saw that he must play his part, as we all must play our part — only she more perfectly.

In the forty days between Christ's ascension into heaven and the descent of the Holy Spirit, we learn (Acts 1:13) that there was what appears to have been a daily meeting of the Apostles in the Upper Room, the room of the Last Supper. "All these with one accord devoted themselves to prayer, together with the women and Mary, the mother of Jesus, and with his brethren." This is the first time we hear of Mary with the Apostles — "(the company of persons was in all about a hundred and twenty)." "When the day of Pentecost had come they were all together in one place . . . and there appeared to them tongues of fire, distributed and resting on each of them. And they were all filled with the Holy Spirit" (2:1-4).

If the key events in Redemption are Christ's birth in Bethlehem, His entry into public life at Cana, His death on Calvary, and the Church's baptism in the Holy Spirit and in fire at Pentecost, she is present at all of them; and we hear no word from her at any of them. But one towering word we hear about her — "God sent his Son, born of a woman." So said Paul to the Galatians (4:4). Alone in all the world she could say to God the Father, "Your Son and mine." I wonder if she ever did.

Paul wrote this around 50 A.D., a good dozen years before Luke's Gospel was written, or the Greek version of Matthew, both of which tell of Christ's birth of a virgin. Luke was Paul's companion and Paul must have read his Gospel while he was writing it. But the Galatians phrase was already written. We think this utterance by Paul suggests that Mary had already died. To report a virgin birth of a living woman would have had both Jewish and Roman leaders on the prowl.

Given that Christ is the representative man, it is clear that what was completed in Him must be repeated in men. And in fact we find it so. There is no element in His humanity or His actions or His suffering that we do not find — not exactly mirrored in the lives of His followers, but happening in them in a way that does seem to mirror their reality in Him.

In His mother this is evident in small matters as in great. The last words we hear from her, as we have noted, are, "Do whatever he tells you." It was her rule of life, much like His, "My will is to do the will of him that sent me." Paul links man's duty of obedience with Christ's — "He learnt obedience by the things he suffered. And being made perfect, he became the means of salvation to all who obey him" (Hebrews 5:8-9). His passion brought Him to perfection; her desolation is parallel, in itself and in its effectiveness. He suffered to the limit of possibility, but could her suffering on Calvary have fallen far below His? — any mother who has watched a child suffer will know what I mean. At least it left no element in Mary or her Son not caught in the fierceness of its flame.

In small things too, we see her desolation paralleled with His passion as a kind of com-passion. He cried on Calvary: "My God, My God why have you forsaken me?" That cry carries an echo of hers uttered so long before, "Son, why have you done this to us?" What had He done to them? Separated Himself.

Each can make his own list of these parallels. These have struck me; others may strike you more powerfully. There is one greater thing we might overlook. So many of the Jewish people repudiated Him; so many Christian people have repudiated her. This repudiation, at least, seems to be changing. So may that earlier one.

We have noted the last words we have from her. There is pleasure in remembering the last sight we have of her — in the upper room, praying, while His followers prayed, waiting for Pentecost.

Postscript to Chapter Four

This book's first chapter was not a study of my wife, but only of her "heart," in the Scripture sense of that word — the combination of intellect and will from which her decisions flowed. This chapter on Our Lady is written within the same limitations. It is my effort to *meet* her as the virgin mother of the Second Person of the Blessed Trinity, to examine the situations in which she made the great decisions and what the decisions themselves meant to her.

I have written elsewhere of her place in the History of Salvation — as the second Eve; of her Immaculate Conception and her Assumption; of how the Church has grown in awareness of her as Christ's mother and ours; of the extraordinary attraction she has exercised over all types of men and women in the fantastic variations of human life from century to century. I am concerned here only with her heart and the light it sheds on our own lesser hearts.

At the end of the Middle Ages there grew up in France a devotion to Our Lady's swoon at the foot of the cross. The Pope, that very belligerent person Julius II, was asked to make it a feast of the whole Church. He consulted the notable Dominican Cardinal Cajetan: the answer was a flat negative. That particular devotion was an example of reading one's own heart into hers! We cannot know how one would react who had had grace in her soul from the instant of her conception, had willed always what God willed, had had thirty years of shared life with God-made-man. If we had not studied the Christ of Scripture and Liturgy we might see Him on Calvary as victim only, and we might be brought near swooning by His sufferings.

But these things were only Calvary's surface.

He was Priest as well as Victim, and He was effecting mankind's redemption. He knew it; His Mother would have known it from Him. She had not climbed Calvary's hill to fail her Son at the peak at once of His agony and His achievement. That He was aware of her, right to the very moment of His death, we know from His giving her to be John's mother and, as we believe, ours.

I do not mean that emotion is meaningless or valueless. One might have mastered and accepted the whole Gospel message — seeing and accepting Christ's will for us as the rule of life, seeing what Mary meant to Him and so to us — with no emotional reaction at all. Temperaments vary: some may over-react to feeling; some may feel little or nothing. We have glanced at people to whom feeling is all. What of the other extreme? I may be wrong in seeing Wordsworth's sonnet to the

Mother of God as an example. Everyone knows the wonderful line in which he hails Mary as

Our tainted nature's solitary boast.

The sonnet has no other line to match that, nor any which has lived in public memory. Yet it is a magnificent statement of Mary as Virgin and Mother, sinless — written thirty years before Rome's definition of the Immaculate Conception. Wordsworth has himself defined poetry as "emotion recollected in tranquility." So perhaps there had been no very strong emotion for him to recollect.

Meeting Mary in the Gospels, in the teaching of the Church, in the Liturgy, in the Rosary, we find her motherhood putting on for us the reality which belongs to it, becoming part of the individual world each person has. This is made up of the people who and the things which, for good or ill, really matter to us — parents, children, employers, personal or national situations, the people we work with, play with, travel with, like or fear. We do not set out to *impose* a personal relation on any of these people. The relation makes itself, gradually perhaps, anything from mere awareness to fascination. Our religious life is healthy if Christ and His mother are members of our individual world. If He is a living person to us and she is not, we are missing a deep element in Him. If she is living to us and He barely known, then we have got her badly wrong. In the physical order He got His life from her; in the order of grace, she gets hers from Him. And we are all one Body, with His grace as its living element.

In the Body the strength of one helps the weakness of another, above all by prayer. In the prayer He gave us as a model, He establishes this clearly — not "give *me* this day my daily bread, forgive *me* my trespasses, deliver *me* from evil," but "give *us*, forgive *us*, deliver *us*." Our Lord wills that we pray not for ourselves only but for others as well. Paul urges (1 Timothy 2:1-5) "that supplications, prayers, intercessions, thanksgivings may be made for all men," this because "there is one mediator between God and men, the man Christ Jesus." Thus he asked the Thessalonians (2.3:1-2): "Pray for us . . . that we may be delivered from wicked and evil men. . . ."

So we ask Our Lady to pray for our spiritual needs. There is a wonderful letter written to G. K. Chesterton by Hilaire Belloc, after a conversation about Chesterton's possible conversion. Here is some of it:

> If we differed on all main points I would not write this, but there are one or two on which we agree. One is Vere passus, immolatus in cruce pro homine.* Another is in looking up to our Dear Lady, the blessed Mother of God.

> I recommend to you this, that you suggest to her a comprehension for yourself of what indeed is the permanent home of the soul. If it is here, you will see it; if it is there, you will see it.

---

*He [Christ] truly suffered and was slain in sacrifice on the cross for man.

He ends:

> *My point is: If it is right, she knows. If it is not right,*
> *she knows.*

Maisie and I had both men for friends. Belloc *knew* how close Our Lady is to us. So did Maisie. Chesterton came to know it. In my way I know it as they did.

What in essence does her motherhood mean to us? I have already suggested that many of her devotees seem to feel actual thinking unnecessary: love is enough. They have certainly let themselves go. I remember a lecturer urging me to call Mary "Mama"! I remember a small boy, under the influence doubtless of some such lecturer, dismissing his own mother as "just a babysitter for Our Lady." She is indeed our Mother-by-adoption as Christ is our Brother-by-adoption — each in the supernatural order, the order of grace and salvation. But grace has no direct access to our emotions — only indirect access through its effect upon the self from which the emotions flow. People who feel that love is to be measured by what it makes us feel emotionally, who are miserable because they cannot feel miserable enough about Christ's agony in the garden, are driven to say the kind of things I have just quoted.

My mother was not an inadequate substitute for Christ's Mother, any more than my brother was for Christ. When my brother died I missed him no less acutely because I still had Christ. My care for my mother's sufferings got no comfort from the thought that Christ's mother suffered worse. The categories are different, and our reactions to them gain nothing by crisscrossing — as when a mother demands from a son the kind of devotion she never got from his father. I think a lot of the emotionalism about Mary came from people who had not been rightly related to their own mothers — either untouched by their love or smothered by it. I love Our Lady better for having had a superb mother to introduce her to me.

All this in the order of her spiritual motherhood. What of physical things? There is usually a spiritual component even in them; in this you are invariably aided, in the rest surprisingly often! You reach a point of familiarity with her, you discuss everything with her.

Talking of Belloc, I remember a stanza from the poem "In a Little Boat." I cannot end this book better:

> *My body is frozen,*
> *My soul is afraid.*
> *Reach out your hand to me,*
> *Mother and maid.*

Beyond counting are the millions through the ages who in their own way of speech have said just that to her.

INDEX: PEOPLE, PLACES, BOOKS